# TEENS AND Devil-Worship

## What Everyone Should Know



Charles G. B. Evans

HUNTINGTON HOUSE PUBLISHERS

Huntington House Publishers
P.O. Box 53788
Lafayette, Louisiana 70505

Library of Congress Card Catalog Number
91-72962
ISBN 1-56384-004-9

# Dedication

*to:*
*. . .my parents, who, like Jesus,*
*continued to love me even when*
*I was unlovable.*

*. . .and to my wife, who, like Jesus,*
*loves me in spite of my past.*

# Contents

# Foreword

Sacrifice can be such a positive word. When it refers to the selfless giving of one person to another, it describes the best of being human. And when it describes what Jesus Christ did for we humans, it describes the best of God Himself. Sacrifice also describes a large part of what parenting means. What a great, God-given privilege it is to give the best of ourselves to nurture and mature a part of ourselves.

But sacrifice also has a "dark side," especially in regard to parenting. In our culture, where values are topsy-turvy, sacrificing for our children has tragically degenerated into sacrificing of our children—at the altars of our own selfishness, convenience, and apathy. If our kids can't come to us because we aren't there, they will find someone to run to. And the growing numbers of "deserted" kids—kids to whom home is little more than a place to sleep and eat—have fuelled occult influences in this country in a way we could never have imagined. We've left too many of our kids on Satan's doorstep.

Charles Evans knows the despair that comes from pinning your hopes on the enemy. As a teenage Satanist, he was driven to the brink of suicide before Jesus Christ mercifully invaded his life and delivered him from the lies of the occult. In the past decade he has spoken to thousands of teenagers and parents about how insidiously easy it is for a kid to buy the lies of Satan when there is no one there to tell him or her the truth. And his experience is balanced with scholarship about the occult and, more important, scholarship in the Word of God.

The pages of Charles' book are filled with hope—both for kids slowly suffocating under the burden of the occult, and for their parents, who suddenly realize that their kids' "weird" interests are more than just passing fads. That hope is rooted in Jesus Christ, for only He is “the way, the truth, and the life” as Charles learned firsthand. As I have come to know Charles, I know he will be satisfied only if the readers of his book are pointed back to Christ. And that is as it should be.

Read this book carefully. It is the voice of experience. Apply its principles diligently. They come from God’s Word. Love your kids fervently. They truly are “a gift of the Lord” (Psalm 127:3).

Perry Brown
Editor/American Tract Society
Garland, Texas

# Acknowledgments

This book would not have been possible without the assistance, encouragement, and support of countless individuals far too numerous to mention by name.

However, I would be remiss if I failed to mention the following friends whose frequent and reliable counsel continually spurred me forward.

Special heartfelt thanks are extended to . . .

Perry Brown/American Tract Society

Peter Lalonde/*Omega Letter & Christian World Report*

Dr. Cecil Johnson/Christian Bible College

Dr. Jack Van Impe/Jack Van Impe Ministries,

and most importantly, I am sincerely grateful to the Lord for allowing me the privilege of serving Him through the writing of *Teens and Devil-Worship: What Everyone Should Know.*

# 1

# I WAS A TEEN-AGE SATANIST

*I almost killed myself. I was seventeen-years-old and had been involved in the occult and Satan worship for approximately two years. I thought suicide was the only way out.*

* * * * * * *

There are several books on the market dealing with the current popularity of Satanism and the problems, both legal and social, which it often fosters. So why write another?

The reasons for this book are many and varied, but the main one is the simple fact that I've been there. I know what the kids are going through. I understand why many of them think that Satanism *must be* better than Christianity. I can relate to their desire for a more exciting spiritual experience than what the average church offers. I also know that contrary to what the Satanists believe and teach, there really is a way out.

Perhaps the best way to begin this project is by sharing my own personal testimony. To do so, I need to take you back into my childhood. You see, my involvement with devil worship didn't "just happen" when I turned fifteen. For me, the groundwork had been laid well in advance.

* * * * * * *

I was born into and raised in a good Christian family. That is, I always thought we were good Christians. After all, no one in the family had a criminal record, we were polite and fairly thoughtful. And we did the proper Christian things: we went to church every Sunday, said prayers before meals, and had the standard twenty-pound family Bible conspicuously displayed on the coffee table and conveniently protected by a thin layer of dust.

So how could such a cute little guy from a good, church-going family end up involved with the devil? Actually, the church we attended kind of helped in that regard. . . . You see, I was an energetic kid. I always had to be doing something, couldn't just sit for an hour listening to a sermon. While I sat in the pew dreaming of playing "cops and robbers" or a long game of baseball after the service, I truly believe my subconscious mind was beginning to formulate the conclusion that there had to be more to "God" than what I was experiencing.

Occasionally my parents would send me downstairs to join the other children in Sunday school. Unfortunately, this too was an exercise in futility since we generally did nothing more than draw pictures or create masterpieces with water paints—kind of a craft and hobby club for Christian kids.

As I think back to those days, I realize just how deficient that particular church really was. Not once was I encouraged to take the Word of God seriously. Not once was I taught to memorize Scripture. Not once was I told of my desperate need of a personal relationship with Jesus.

It became more and more difficult for me to endure the uninteresting, lifeless, tedious church services with every passing week. I remember literally begging my parents to let me stay with the neighbors every once in a while rather than going to church. I just couldn't see the sense of going to church week after week, singing the same songs, praying the same prayers, falling asleep. I couldn't understand why it was so important for me to be there when I didn't seem to be learning anything.

As soon as I was old enough to do so, I told my

parents that I didn't want to go to church anymore. I explained how difficult it was for me to sit through the sermons. I told them that I didn't feel I was benefiting by attending. I told them how much I hated it. And that was that. . . . For a while.

The next step came one evening a few years later. I had always had a love for music, mainly top ten or current hits. It became a regular daily occurrence for friends from school or from the neighborhood to come to my house after supper and listen to records and tapes for hours on end. No problem with that . . . right?

But one night a friend brought over an album by a group called KISS. He was really beginning to like the band, and he wanted me to hear some of their stuff. I put the record on, turned up the volume, and when the music started I turned to my friend with an amazed look on my face and said "You actually *like* this?"

This was my first exposure to heavy metal music, and I wasn't impressed. However, after listening to the album for half an hour or so, I was hooked. The funny part of it was, if you had asked me the day before what I thought of that type of music I wouldn't have had a single good thing to say about it, and I never would have thought that I would begin spending hundreds of dollars on albums, T-shirts, rock posters and magazines, concert tickets, and constantly improving stereo equipment!

The music was almost like a drug. Beginning with nothing more than a brief taste of it, I eventually ended up addicted, quite literally. Rock-and-roll quickly began to control my life. It got to the point that I hated to be anywhere if I couldn't have my music (e.g., doctor's or dentist's offices, family gatherings).

Naturally this became quite a problem for me where school was concerned. It actually became very difficult for me to go to school because I would necessarily have to be without my music for several hours. This detail alone caused me to begin feigning sickness and skipping classes just so I could be home with my beloved stereo. From the time I got up in the morning to the time I went to bed, rock music had to be there.

I recall a particularly stormy winter night when I had to shovel snow and ice from the driveway. I felt as though I couldn't possibly accomplish such a task without my music, so I joined several heavy-duty extension cords together and plugged in my portable cassette player, which was protected from the falling snow by a plastic bread bag. (This was before the tiny cassette players with headphones were available.)

Another method of getting my music fix was to attach my tape player to the handlebars of my ten-speed bike with yards and yards of electrical tape and fill my pockets with a good supply of batteries. I have since come to learn that my dependency on rock-and-roll music was not a unique problem. Countless teen-agers are faced with the same symptoms and ill-effects today. But we'll talk more about this later.

Quite a number of preachers say that the problem with rock music is the beat. This may very well be in some cases, but my problems started with the lyrics.

Slowly I began to notice that all of my favorite groups sang a lot about the occult—witchcraft, magic, the devil—and when I first realized it, it bothered me. But then I started to purposely listen to what some of these songs were saying. It seemed to me that these artists truly believed what they were singing about. It seemed as though they felt confident about their religious views. I couldn't help but wonder if maybe they had found the right religion since the one I was raised with was a dismal failure in my eyes.

It was a simple task to find books at the local book stores and public libraries that described many of the terms and names I was hearing in the music I listened to. Although I never intentionally set out to become involved in the occult, and that point is important, my curiosity kept urging me on to learn more and more about it.

It wasn't long before I was seriously studying everything I could get my hands on that dealt with the black arts in any way, shape, or form. I think it's important to point out that my initial involvement in the occult came by way of so-called white magic or white witchcraft. I truly believed that I wasn't doing anything displeasing to God since I prayed to the "Queen of Heaven" and only performed ceremonies to help people.

As is often the case, however, this "pure magic" proved to be unsatisfying and served as nothing more than an introduction to the darker side of the occult arts. As so many others before and after me, I deduced that black magic would probably be more intense, more exciting, more powerful, and more rewarding.

I immersed myself in books on several different aspects of magic and the supernatural, and before too long, I had my own collection of books on witchcraft, vodoun (more commonly, voodoo), necromancy, astrology, seances, and so on.

I began performing spells and rituals on a more frequent basis. I was absolutely thrilled to be so actively involved in my religion. This was so much better than just sitting in a pew Sunday after Sunday!

But then, you guessed it, I grew tired of black magic. There had to be more out there. And then it came to me; if black magic was this exciting, this fascinating, this powerful, why not go directly to the source of the power and plug into it!

Although I never consciously set out to become involved in Satanism in any way, I eventually wound up believing in the devil, praying to the devil and ultimately, worshipping the devil.

This is perhaps one of the most important things for the kids who are considering dabbling in the occult to understand—a great many young people who become deeply involved in Satanism and end up committing heinous crimes like rape, murder, or suicide, did not start off with such plans.

I liken this to what I consider to be the perfect analogy—experimenting with drugs. How many kids have started off small, maybe with booze on the weekend or an occasional joint now and then, and later decide that they want to try something with a little more "kick"? Eventually they end up trying cocaine or crack and find that they just can't walk away from it no matter how much they might want to.

So often occult involvement is exactly the same. Most people can't just "taste it" and walk away. It just isn't that easy. The change is so gradual that the person involved may not even notice what is happening to him/her.

Jim Hardy, a young man currently serving a life sentence with no chance of parole for the murder of his friend, Steve Newberry, as a "sacrifice to Satan" simply says, "You can't just mess around. It sucks you in."[1]

Of course, all of this interest in the occult caused me to become even more of a rock music fan. I especially appreciated the bands that used satanic symbols on their album covers and sang about the devil. The more sinister the band appeared and the more they sang about Satan, the better I liked them.

Obviously, this formed a vicious circle. My love for satanic rock music continually fuelled my interest in the occult while my interest in the occult influenced me to listen to more and more satanic music.

One of the most interesting aspects of the music I was listening to at that time was the fact that these groups were definitely doing their homework. They were not simply making up names and titles and symbols that looked or sounded cultish. Rather, the names of various rituals or fetishes, and other details were quite accurate. In fact, in the beginning I gathered most of my knowledge of the occult by looking up various words and titles I heard in the songs.

This causes me to question those bands that claim they are not personally involved in Satanism or the occult but simply use it as a gimmick to sell records. The problem with this however, is that whether or not the band members really are involved in worshipping the devil, thousands of kids *think* that they are, and consequently they deduce that if it's O.K. for their favorite rock idols, it's O.K. for them.

But back to my story. . . . I have to admit that during the time I was involved in Satanism, I often felt pangs of doubt about what I was doing. As I mentioned, I was raised in a pseudo-Christian home and was taught to be good and kind and live by the golden rule.

Of course, one of the first laws of Satanism is completely contrary to such ideals. Satanism is a very selfish religion and its adherents are encouraged to do whatever they choose to do. In fact, this is one of the main lures to many who become involved with it. There are no moral rules, no lists of "Don'ts." If one chooses to lie, cheat, or steal, he or she is free to do so. If a Satanist wants to hurt others in his quest for power, fame, or fortune, he does so.

It should be immediately obvious that such a structure, if we may use such a complimentary title, is far more appealing to many teen-agers than the monstrous and ever-growing list of rules that we Christians seem to feel we must lay upon the backs of others.

Whenever such doubts would begin to tug at my conscience they were quickly chased away by simple reasoning: "Satan must be stronger than God since it is clear by the condition of the world that he (Satan) is in control" or "Hell will only be a place of torment for those who do not serve Satan on the earth. For those who do, it will be an endless party."

It should be duly noted that such faulty reasoning would not be so wide-spread today if the Body of Christ was preaching and teaching the truths of the Word of God rather than watering down its message with liberal opinions and traditions.

At any rate, there was one persistent reality that I

was never able to deny, and it was this factor that ultimately drew me to a saving knowledge of the Lord Jesus Christ.

After I had been involved in the occult and Satanism for approximately a year and a half, my father was admitted to the local hospital for some routine surgery. His roommate was a born-again believer. Although my Dad had gone to church consistently, read the Bible, and certainly believed in the existence of the Lord, it became clear to him that this gentleman who shared his hospital room had something he didn't.

The visitors that my Dad's new friend had daily were also believers. They made it a practice to share the Gospel with my father, read the Bible to him, and pray with him. I remember going to the hospital one afternoon to visit Dad. As usual there were several people in the room—all Christians—and I, of course, was the only devil-worshipper!

My Dad introduced me to one of his new friends who proceeded to shake my hand with the force of a small earthquake and smile with a grin that threatened to rip the edges of his mouth. He looked me right in the eye and said, "Jesus loves you."

Boy, did I get a wicked case of the uncomfortables! I hated this guy for saying that to me! Who did he think he was anyway? The nerve of the guy—to say such a thing as "Jesus loves you" to a total stranger, a Satanist! But I could never get that out of my head. This man seemed to have such a peace and genuine happiness in him. He definitely had whatever it was that I was missing. And I wanted it.

Before he was discharged from the hospital, my father accepted the Lord Jesus as his personal Saviour and Lord and became a brand new creation! (2 Cor. 5:17).

Can you imagine our household when Daddy came home? Picture if you will a miserable, moody, long-haired, devil-worshipping kid with a huge hexagram on the basement floor and an altar to Satan complete with black-handled knives, candles, and other occult paraphernalia while upstairs you have a brand-new, born-again, Bible-believing, blood-bought, sin-hatin', Jesus-lovin' babe in the Lord with a stupid grin on his face and a peace in his heart that nearly drove me right 'round the bend!

This is when the fun began. You see, up till then my parents just figured that my addiction to satanic rock music, my long hair, and my obsession with the occult was nothing more than a passing fad or a period of normal teen-age rebellion. But when Daddy got saved, that started a whole new ball game! All of a sudden, fad or no fad, he just wasn't gonna have any Satanism in his house and that was that!

Although my Dad was a brand-new believer there was one thing he learned about real quick and that was the power of prayer. Dad began praying for me, and before I knew it, just about every Christian in the city was asking the Lord to show me the errors of my ways and draw me unto Himself. I wasn't aware of their prayers at the time, but there was certainly one thing *I was aware of*, that nagging feeling of doubt and uncertainty was back with a vengeance!

With each and every passing day I felt worse and worse about myself. It got to the point where I dreaded getting out of bed in the morning because I just didn't have any reason to get up. There was no purpose in my life, no reason for living. I had grown into the kind of person I had never wanted to be—a long-haired, miserable, unemployed, booze hound with a ferocious temper.

I began to feel that if I could just break off my involvement with Satanism, I could get my life back together. But that's where it got complicated. Every book on Satanism I had ever read spelled it out quite clearly: Once you set your foot on the path, *there is no turning back—ever.*

When I first casually mentioned to a friend of mine, who had also become involved in the occult, that I was toying with the idea of leaving it, he sternly warned me that I better not even think about it. But it wasn't long before he actually came to me and said that he too was growing more and more uncomfortable about what we were playing with. But what could we do? Because the idea that one can never leave Satanism was consistently drilled into our heads from every imaginable source, we came to the conclusion that death would be the only way out.

I will never forget the night that we drove to the Niagara River and just stood there on the bank cursing ourselves for ever being foolish enough to get mixed up in such stupidity. It may be hard for those who have never actually seen Niagara Falls or the Niagara River to picture the seriousness of our intentions. Suffice it to say that once you're in it, you don't come out—at least not alive. I remember looking at my friend and fellow Satanist and saying, "It's hard to believe that in about five minutes we're gonna be in hell forever."

To this day I have no idea why we didn't carry out our plans. We were standing right by the river's edge. We had concluded that suicide was our only escape. But we didn't do it. And the pattern continued. I struggled through each day feeling worse than the day before. I could hardly stand the sight of myself in the mirror. What in the world was causing me to feel so filthy?

It all came together early one morning as I was driving home from yet another party. As I drove along the sparsely lit back roads, I began to cry. And I felt like an absolute idiot! What was I crying about? Nothing had happened. I hadn't been thinking about anything in particular. I wasn't injured. The tears started flowing in a torrent, actual gut-wrenching sobs that made it necessary for me to pull off the road and park for a few minutes. I cried out to Satan and asked him what was happening. But there was no answer. I prayed to him asking him to give me strength and to take away this horrible feeling of weakness, emptiness. Nothing.

I told him that I was sorry for even considering leaving him and that if he would just give me some relief from these feelings of uselessness, guilt, and confusion I would re-dedicate myself to him and serve him as I never had before. I heard nothing but silence.

Soon after giving my life to Jesus and being freed from the bondage of the enemy, I learned two things. First of all, I had experienced these constantly increasing feelings of despair and helplessness because the Holy Spirit of God was dealing with my heart and letting me know that my life wasn't right. Why was He doing this? Because Christians were praying.

Secondly, the devil didn't respond to any of my pleas that night as I wept because he couldn't. The Lord was dealing with me and drawing me into a saving knowledge of Himself and, although I certainly didn't believe it at the time, He is much stronger than Satan and wouldn't allow him to interfere with what He was doing. But I'm getting ahead of myself. . . .

After several minutes of desperately trying to figure out what in the world was happening, I was able to regain my composure and drive the rest of the way home. When I got there I headed straight for my bedroom, fell down by my bed, and cried out to God. I didn't know if He could hear me. I didn't know if He could help me. I didn't even know *if He would* help me. But I had reached the bottom, and I had no where else to look but up.

Asking the Lord to save me was probably one of the most difficult things I have ever done because, as I mentioned earlier, I had been conditioned to believe that to do so was to sign my death certificate. I truly and honestly believed with all my heart that the devil himself was going to come into my room that night and take my life.

But he didn't . . . because he couldn't. And that's why I've written this book—to tell young people that Satan is a liar and that regardless of what you may have read or heard, there is a way to be freed from his grip.

# 2

# DO PEOPLE REALLY WORSHIP THE DEVIL?

*". . . . If the hundreds of newspaper headlines, police reports, and personal testimonies of parents, children, teenagers and adult survivors across this country and around the world are even partially true, then we are being inundated with satanic and ritualistic practices and beliefs on an unprecedented scale."*[1]

Johanna Michaelsen

* * * * * * *

Over the years Hollywood has led many to believe that the devil is a hideously ugly creature with red skin, black eyes, cloven hooves dagger-like fangs and horns. He has been portrayed by artists as a half human/half animal mutation resembling that which only our most terrifying nightmares could design.

But no where in the Bible do we find such descriptions of Satan. In fact, quite the opposite is true. The Old Testament describes him before he fell from heaven and clearly states that he was full of wisdom and perfect in beauty (Ezek. 28:12). We are also told that he was covered with exquisite jewels and stones (v. 13). Interestingly enough, although few seem to realize it, the Word of God does not say that Lucifer instantly became grotesque and repulsive when he was cast out of heaven. Rather, we are told that he is capable of appearing as an attractive angel of light (2 Cor. 11:14).

This is tremendously important. Simple logic tells us that the average person is not tempted by anything that tastes dreadful, smells terrible, or appears unattractive. Instead, we are tempted by those things that are delicious, smell heavenly, and are pleasing to the eyes.

For example, if I was to place a heaping plate of rotten seaweed in front of you, would you be at all tempted to eat any of it? Of course not! On the other hand, what if I replaced that dish with a scrumptious piece of cherry cheesecake? You'd dig right in! Similarly, Satan is able to effectively tempt so many to follow him because he makes his offers sound *so good.*

Naturally, if Satan presented the real facts to those he tempts, the vast majority would want nothing to do with him. After all, who really wants to end up on death row because they followed the devil's instructions to murder their family members? Who really wants to beat a friend to death with a baseball bat in a satanically inspired frenzy? Who really wants to end up as an unwilling human sacrifice to Satan? But again, he makes it look so good.

Keeping the above in mind, the next logical question is *Why*. Why does anyone decide to worship the devil? As with many aspects of Satanism among teen-agers, this question cannot be answered with a single, straightforward reply. In actual fact, there are several different reasons why an individual may decide to follow Satan.

Here are some of the main reasons:

**Subtle or blatant enticement through heavy metal rock music**—As we shall see later in this book, there can be no doubt that rock music, particularly "heavy metal" and "black metal" rock, has a very definite and very strong drawing power over teen-agers today. As I mentioned in the preceding chapter, my own involvement with the occult and Satanism as a teen-ager was brought on by two contributing factors, one of which was the fact that my favorite rock-and-roll artists sang so much about the subjects. The other contributing factor in my case was . . .

**A lack of fulfillment with traditional religious practices**—The Bible declares that the Kingdom of God "is not in word, but in power" (1 Cor. 4:20). Unfortunately, the Christian Church has largely forgotten or is busy denying this important truth. It is instead promulgating a false impression that causes millions of teen-agers all over the United States and Canada to assume that the Christian religion is best suited to the elderly and/or those who simply have nothing better to do with their time.

My eventual interest in the black arts had its beginning, although I was unaware of it at the time, way back in the church I attended with my family. The important doctrinal truths of the Bible were never taught, the exciting, life-changing Gospel was never presented, and as a result, I concluded that Christianity couldn't be "the right religion" since there simply had to be more to God than falling asleep in a church pew every Sunday morning.

The sad part of this example is that I am not the only young person who reached this erroneous conclusion. Many teen-agers I have personally encountered are experiencing exactly the same doubts and questions about Christianity. The Church seems intent on hiding the power and truth of the Gospel in its attempt to remain socially acceptable in the nineties.

**Movies, videos, books, etc. presenting occult/satanic themes**—Along with black metal music, an incredibly large number of movies, videos, books (including comic books) dealing with the occult and the supernatural are enjoying a tremendous surge in popularity among today's teen-agers.

It is interesting to note that while horror movies and fictional novels about ghouls and ghosts have been popular for quite some time, a noticeable difference can be seen between traditional horror thrillers like *Frankenstein* or *The Mummy* and the popular titles today like *Witchboard*, *The Unholy* and *The Gate*.

While *Frankenstein* dealt with a fictional monster, which was constructed from wires, bolts, and various spare parts, the top horror movies today invariably deal with occult themes—calling up demons through black magic rituals, selling one's soul to the devil, or even ritualistic sacrifices to Satan.

The main problem with movies such as these is that, more often than not, the rituals and ceremonies performed in the movies are completely accurate when compared to actual witchcraft and/or satanic rituals.

After watching "Superman" fly on television, many youngsters tied makeshift capes around their necks and dove out of windows. Similarly, kids today are experimenting with occult rituals they see in movies, having no comprehension of just how damaging the results can be.

At the risk of sounding paranoid, it should also be mentioned here that many children's toys as well as Saturday morning cartoons are now based on occult themes.

I will never forget the feeling I had as my wife and I watched a popular children's cartoon one morning. I sat in stunned amazement as a prominent character in the story performed the same occult ritual that I had performed many times myself as a practicing Satanist!

It is imperative that parents comprehend the seriousness of this problem. If one or two cartoons casually mentioned witchcraft, demons, or the occult once in a while, I'd say not to be too terribly worried. But when one cartoon after the other blatantly fills our children's minds with occult terminology, extremely unbalanced theology, and actual black magic rituals, we definitely have something to be concerned about!

**Simple curiosity**—Many kids, and many adults for that matter, toy with various aspects of the occult simply because they are intrigued by it. They may have no desire or intention of ever actually becoming a practicing witch or Satanist, they just want to know a little bit more about the subject. Does magic really work? Can I really cast spells? Is it possible to talk to the dead? Which of us hasn't wondered these same things from time to time.

For some, however, their interest extends beyond wondering about the occult. Countless people choose to involve themselves with that which they know little or nothing about fully believing that it will be a simple matter to just back out if they lose interest or become frightened. But it isn't that easy.

As mentioned earlier, I like to compare occult involvement with drug experimentation. Consider the thousands upon thousands of unfortunate souls who tried marijuana a few times and liked it and then couldn't help but try to find an even bigger thrill from a stronger drug. The problem is that the stronger drugs are highly addictive. Once you've had that first little taste, you feel as though you *must* have more. This progression continues until the user who was "just curious" to begin with becomes hopelessly and helplessly hooked on the very thing that he was sure he could control.

Occult involvement is the same. One may start out doing a basic ceremony once in a while, but before too long, he finds himself wanting to learn more, wanting to do more. Occult involvement is something that must be completely avoided at all costs. *The black arts are nothing to play with!*

**Peer pressure**—This phenomena, peer pressure, is responsible for leading countless kids into trouble in numerous areas. There can be no doubt that most kids start smoking cigarettes because everyone else does and you just aren't cool if you don't. Kids get into alcohol and drugs because everyone else is doing it. Kids get involved in gangs because their friends are, and they want to fit in. And lately kids are getting involved in Satanism because everyone else seems to be doing it.

Peer pressure is an incredibly difficult thing. Like

anyone of any age, kids desperately want to be accepted by their peers. And why not? Does anyone really want to be left completely alone, with no friends, no companions, no acknowledgment? Unfortunately, many of the kids who get into Satanism for this reason may not even want to be involved in it. The very thought of it may disturb them greatly. But they are willing to go to great lengths to be part of the crowd.

**Rebellion against parental and/or social authorities**—It seems as though a certain amount of rebelliousness is expected from every generation of teen-agers. It was evident in the fifties when rock-and-roll music began raising quite a few adult eyebrows, and it is obvious today through vandalism, violence, flag-burning and, of course, Satanism.

Although it would be a mistake to label *all* satanic involvement among young people as simple rebellion, there can be little doubt that many of the kids who are desecrating cemeteries, spray-painting occult symbols on buildings and bridges, or abusing neighborhood pets are doing so for no better reason than to voice their opposition to parental and/or civil authorities. Of course, years ago a teen-ager could show his or her seditiousness simply by smoking a cigarette or muttering a four-letter word. As we'll see later however, kids need to do a lot more than that just to be noticed today.

**Need or desire to be noticed**—Sadly, many kids risk their futures, their families, even their very lives by messing around with Satanism because they have reached the conclusion that it is the only way to get the attention of their parents. Parents seem to have to deal with endless pressures and worries. Such concerns seem to increase when both parents are busy with full-time jobs. Consequently, kids are discovering that they have to do something "really bad" just to let the rest of the world know that they're around.

**A desperate appeal for attention or help**—Unfortunately, some kids might want more than attention from their parents, they might truly need help from them. It is not unheard of for kids to resort to drastic measures when they are confused or scared and can't seem to get that message across to their parents by conventional methods. Lately these "drastic measures" have included satanic activities.

**Empty promises of sexual, material, or spiritual fulfillment**—In this day and age of greed, lust, and the almighty dollar, the devil is able to attract countless followers by promising them whatever they desire in exchange for their souls. The Bible, however, describes Satan as a liar. There are many people in prisons today who would be quick to agree with that statement. Many of those who have been convicted of committing atrocious crimes in the name of Satan had truly believed that he (Satan) would protect them from any and all consequences of their actions. The kids need to be shown that once he gets what he wants, the devil immediately breaks his deals without carrying out his part of the bargain.

The bottom line here is that Satan couldn't care less what happens to those who follow him. He hates all mankind with a vengeance and trusting him to make good on anything he says is foolhardy to say the least.

**Power**—The sense of personal power is perhaps one of the strongest drawing cards of contemporary Satanism. Many young people feel that the condition of the world indicates that Satan, and not God, is in control. Satanism provides some kids with something to believe in, something that might not be viewed as clean, pure, or white, but something that is certainly dependable and not hypocritical.[2]

**Desire to be like their rock idols**—Lastly, kids may get involved in the black arts even if they are not at all interested in doing so simply because they want to take after their favorite rock musicians. It makes little difference whether or not the performers are truly involved in Satanism. All it takes is for the fan to believe that they are and to want to emulate them.

After considering the main reasons for kids getting involved in the worship of the devil, it may also be wise to point out the different levels of Satanism before going further.

There are four main levels or kinds of Satanism as described below.

**The dabbler**—There can be no doubt that the majority of kids who consider themselves to be "Satanists" would be more accurately classified as dabblers. A dabbler is one who simply fools around with that which he or she *assumes* is satanic while having little or no knowledge or understanding of what literal devil worship entails.

The dabbler is generally not associated with a structured or organized coven. Therefore, he tends to do meaningless things, which have no place in authentic Satanism—things like skinning the neighborhood cat, knocking over tombstones, or spray-painting occult-related symbols on buildings and bridges. The average layperson, however, naively labels such crimes as "satanic."

For the most part these kids are attempting to commit the most vile, disgusting, and offensive atrocities they can dream up erroneously assuming that what is wicked and dirty must naturally be satanic. It is for this reason that I feel the dabbler should be recognized as one of the most serious threats. Because of his lack of structure and authority, the dabbler has been known to go to the extremes of torture and human sacrifice in his quest for the ultimate evil.

We are hearing of more and more kids committing unbelievably vile and perverse crimes in the name of Satan as they attempt to do those things that they believe their "master" would appreciate.

**The self-styled Satanist**—The self-styled Satanist is one who is more serious about his involvement in Satanism and consequently views it as his religion rather than simply imitating scenes from occult movies. Detailed rituals are studied and memorized from books and/or taught by a practicing Satanist as opposed to the dabbler who generally concocts his own peculiar ceremonies, which usually have no resemblance to authentic Satanism.

The self-styled Satanist is probably less likely to carry out the senseless crimes that characterize the dabbler simply because he (the self-styled Satanist) realizes that such practices have no place in genuine devil worship. However, this is not meant to imply that a self-styled worshipper of evil is incapable or unwilling to perform illegal or blasphemous acts if they become necessary to his belief system.

**The public Satanist**—Those who openly promote the satanic religion through books and television appearances are considered "public Satanists." For the most part, such individuals do not promote or endorse any illegal acts that are commonly associated with devil worship (e.g., human or animal sacrifice, torture, etc.). However, this fact should be taken with the proverbial grain of salt as it is painfully obvious that no one could publicly promote such crimes without finding himself in serious legal trouble!

In addition, many of these people run licensed satanic churches or clubs, which would certainly loose their tax-exempt status if illegal acts were found to be part of their activities.

**Hard-core Satanists**—The hard-core Satanist is the most dangerous of all four kinds of devil-worshipper. Belonging to a tight-knit organization, which may include doctors, lawyers, judges and police officers, the hard-core believer is dedicated, heart and soul, to carrying out the goals of his wide-spread group. Human and animal sacrifices are performed on a regular and frequent basis by those involved in this category.

Throughout the remainder of this book, we will be considering the seriousness of Satanism among teen-agers. It is also our aim to provide some practical, albeit sometimes unorthodox, preventative measures to help kids avoid the potential hazards of occult involvement. Lastly, we will suggest steps to be taken in reaching those kids who are already involved in the occult or Satanism.

# 3

# IS THERE REALLY ANYTHING TO WORRY ABOUT?

Before delving into the "whys and wherefores" of Satanism, it may be worthwhile to first establish whether or not there really is a problem. Is satanic involvement among young people as potentially dangerous as some claim? Is Satanism anything more than a localized problem being sensationalized by the media? For that matter, is there really any need for this book?

The following examples should suffice to demonstrate the seriousness of the subject matter at hand:

"CARLETON, MICH.—Lloyd Harold Gamble, 17, was shot and killed in his home at 10600 Otter Creek Rd. about 11:30 A.M. Sunday. Monroe County Sheriff's deputies took a 15-year-old boy into custody at the scene of the shooting.

"Three days after the incident, the investigators had been called by the family and asked to return to the house. The parents said there were some items they wanted them to see. When the investigators got to the house, the parents brought out a green vinyl bag that had been hidden in a closet. It contained a hood, long black robe, silver chalice, dark blue candle, glass bottle containing red liquid, piece of white parchment paper, eleven cassette tapes of Motley Crue, Black Sabbath and other heavy metal groups. There were more items found under a rug. There was a book titled *The Power of Satan*, a paper pentagram, a bingo card (the card had the numbers 666 in a row), a sword, money orders, and an upside-down cross.

"The book, *The Power of Satan*, came from a Satanic group in Canada. We believe he got information about the group while he was at a Motley Crue concert. The book gave step-by-step instructions on how to perform a Satanic ritual. (The book is a nine-page pamphlet reproduced by a copy machine. It bore no copyright holder or author's name, but was sent by a group known as CASH, Continental Association of Satan's Hope, in Montreal.)"[1]

"There was the case of a boy who lived with his very elderly grandmother. He went around the house and took down all of her religious pictures. He took her crucifix and turned it upside down and then beat the hell out of her. Sure, I can't say that he did it because of Satanism, but at the same time school officials were finding all kinds of satanic symbols in his locker. He was making a big deal about letting everyone know that he was involved with Satanism."[2]

"On March 23, 1980, the fifteen year old son of a local official committed suicide by hanging himself in the loft of the residential garage. The deceased was found by a family member at about 0700 hours on 24 March. The youth had covered himself with curious writings that give the appearance of being inspired by cultish connections referencing Satanic origins. Descriptions of markings as follows:

> Upper torso, below base of neck, 'Satan' printed w/orange lipstick. Middle of torso (chest), 'IM COME HOME MASTER' (sic) printed with ball-point pen. Middle lung area, the numbers '666' printed with orange lipstick. Left rib cage area, 'SATAN' printed w/orange lipstick. Front of right leg and ankle, 'I LOVE SATAN' w/ball-point pen. Buttock area, vertical line and, crosswise across

> top of the buttocks, a horizontal line at the bottom of the vertical line. These lines have the appearance of an upside down cross when viewed from top to bottom; this was done w/orange lipstick. Inside of left thigh, 'LUCIFER' printed w/orange lipstick. Blood analysis indicated there was no drugs or toxins present."[3]

"A small group of Northport Harbor, New York, teenagers force student Gary Lauwers to say, 'I love you, Satan' while stabbing him; then they drag him into the woods, gouge out his eyes and leave him to die."[4]

"Seventeen-year-old Theron Roland of Carl's Junction, Missouri, thinks Satan will appear and bless him with power after he and two other teenagers beat a friend to death with baseball bats."[5]

"What was it that possessed fourteen-year-old Tommy Sullivan to tackle his mother to the floor in the basement of his New Jersey home? Possessed by an uncontrollable frenzy, Tommy stabbed his mother fourteen times, slit her throat, slashed most of her face away, and set the house on fire. This likable teenager . . . slit his own wrists and throat with such force that he almost cut his head off.

"The descriptive mandate from his Book of Shadows revealed that he had seen a vision of Satan. In his trance he was ordered to kill his family and preach satanism to his friends."[6]

". . . . Melissa Ernest, seventeen, shrieks as the judge sentences her to life in prison. Teamed with her coven friends, Melissa participated in the human sacrifice of her friend, Theresa Simmons.[7]

"Richard Rameriz, noted Night-Stalker, blurts out 'Hail Satan' in a Los Angeles courtroom. His pentagram tattoo is noticeable on his raised palm."[8]

"On January 6, 1988, popular Vermont sophomore Michelle Kimball killed herself in a suicide pact with her boyfriend. He survived. Her suicide note said that she worshiped Satan and knew her parents wouldn't understand."[9]

"In Roy City, Utah, a youth's satanic oath was found in his billfold after he died of intentional carbon-monoxide poisoning. The handwritten note said: 'In the name of Satan, Lucifer, Belial, Leviathan, and all the demons, named and nameless, walkers in the velvet darkness, harken to us, O dim and shadowy things, wraith-like, twisted, half-seen creatures. Welcome a new and worthy brother.'"[10]

". . . . Four months after a 16-year-old Greenville boy disappeared from a local theater, police found his body in a shallow grave. A 20-year-old indicted for the slaying has been charged with luring the youth to an area, beating him with a club and stabbing him to death.

"The 20-year-old has a 666, known as the mark of Satan, tattooed on his forehead. Police found a robe, black candles, a satanic bible and occult literature in the man's car."[11]

"In Sacramento, California, a 13-year-old girl shot her 11-year-old sister to death. The youngster later sobbed to police that she didn't want to harm her sister, that she was under the control of Satan."[12]

"Terry L. Lowery, 26, is on death row in Michigan City, awaiting execution for the May 1985 murder of 13-year-old Tricia Woods. Lowery has told authorities he is a devil worshiper who hears and sees Satan."[13]

A seven-year-old girl and her parents were shot to death by a fourteen-year-old boy in Toronto, Canada, in 1985. The boy believed that "Eddie," the grotesque mascot of heavy metal band Iron Maiden, had told him that he could achieve freedom by committing the murders. The boy is said to have been dabbling in Satanism and was a fan of Iron Maiden.[14]

A fifteen-year-old boy attacked his father and stabbed him eight times in Ontario, Canada. The boy was said to be under the influences of alcohol, heavy metal music, and a preoccupation with Satan. In British Columbia, Canada, four young girls allegedly carved an inverted cross into the forehead of a fourteen-year-old girl after tying her to a bed. Also in British Columbia, a member of a satanic group died after unknowingly consuming experimental heart drugs during a ritual.[15]

In Brantford, Ontario, a twenty-five-year-old man raped and stabbed his twelve-year-old sister in order to seal a pact he had made with Satan. The man called an ambulance for his sister after the ordeal and explained to the police that he and his brother had been instructed through a Ouija board to commit a murder before Halloween. He claimed that he would have been rewarded if his sister had died.[16]

"Twenty-two year old Joseph Bradsberry was handcuffed with his hands behind his back, stabbed through the throat, beaten and drowned during what was supposed to be an 'initiation' into a loosely organized satanic cult consisting of young drug users and heavy metal music fans.

"The boy identified as leader of the 'coven' was Wallace 'Randy' Ervin, 23. He said Luther Franklin 'Luke' Mays III, 19, and Arthur Odell 'Del' Holley, 26, also joined in the 'ritual' that led to Bradsberry's death. The three young men and a woman, Sandra Colleen Capps, 23, were charged with the murder of Bradsberry."[17]

"GIRL, 13, TOOK PART IN RITUALS. Toronto (CP) A 13-year-old girl who sent threatening letters to her school principal was a member of a group of children who engaged in cult-like activities, says a member of the Metropolitan Toronto Police Youth bureau. Const. Stan Anyan said the girl was one of several children, known to police as the Ravine Gang, who gathered in a north-central Toronto park last year to engage in rituals relating to sex, drugs and alcohol.

"The girl, whose name was not released, sent letters earlier this month to Fred Turner, principal of Glenview Senior Public School, saying she was 'insane enough to kill' and would make the school 'burn in Hell.'

"One of the letters had the word 'Satan' scrawled on the back. Anyan said the girl regularly attended the gatherings which took place almost daily during the spring months last year.

"He said the group once tied a boy to a make-shift cross and danced and chanted around him. Another time, they wore vestments stolen from a nearby church, but fled before police arrived. . . ."

"DEVIL WORSHIPPERS BELIEVED INVOLVED IN CHILD ABDUCTIONS. Calgary (CP) Devil worshippers may have been involved in several unsolved child abduction cases in Alberta, says an RCMP constable who has studied Satanic cults for the last four years.

"'There could be a strong connection between missing children and Satanic cults,' Const. Jim Brown says in a report. 'Children have a strong significance in Satanic rituals and there are suggestions they may be used.'

"Brown, an authority on Satanic cult crimes, said an attempted child kidnapping in Red Deer, Alta., in the summer of 1985 is believed to have been the work of devil worshippers. The attempt coincided with one of 13 annual Satanic holy days, he said.

"Brown writes in his report that Satanic cults are likely responsible for a string of other serious crimes in the Calgary and Red Deer areas since 1982—assaults, extortions, animal mutilations, grave robberies and even 'ritualistic sacrifice of hitchhikers.'

"'Prosecutions of Satanists are rare in Canada because they go to great lengths to avoid detection,' he said. 'You don't get much evidence, because Satanic cults are so clandestine and cover themselves up well.' Children have been the preferred victims of Satanic covens since the Middle Ages, Brown said.

"'Children are basically pure. They aren't corrupt. That fact, for Satanic ritual purposes, is significant. To take a child and use it for a sacrifice is a horrendous thing. But Satanists want to take that child's soul. They want to control it.'

"Rena Kirkham of Childfind Alberta, a group that

tries to locate missing children, said she knows there is a suspected connection between some child abductions and Satanic cults. 'It's definitely possible,' she said."

Certainly the above examples, and countless others which we have neither the space nor the desire to relate, clearly indicate that the enigma of occult and satanic involvement throughout the U.S. and Canada is a matter that must be acknowledged and dealt with.

The following excerpts from letters I have received should serve to reinforce this conclusion.

From a twenty-three-year-old male in Nova Scotia, Canada:

". . . I'm scared. For the last few years I've been listening to heavy metal rock music which I've become addicted to. My favorites are Guns 'n Roses, Wasp, and Ozzy Osbourne. I've also been heavily involved in the occult and Satan worship. I mean, I don't belong to any devil-worshipping church or anything like that. I just worship Satan in my own special room and pray to him and stuff like that.

"Lately though, all I've been able to think of is suicide and I think this is the thing that terrifies me the most because I've never felt like this before and I don't know what to do.

"It's been so many years since I've even set foot into a Christian church. I don't even know who Jesus is anymore, although I still say out loud how I hate him and how much Satan is my master.

"*Please. I need some help, but I just don't know what to do* . . . I feel like I'm at the end of my rope because I just don't know what to do anymore. I'm just burned out and now it seems as if Satan doesn't want me or love me anymore because I'm of no use and that's one of the things which hurts me the most. *Please help me!*"

From a fifteen-year-old female in Pennsylvania:

". . . I was reading your story about when you was young and listening to rock music. Well I'm in the same place you was. I listen to rock music, smoke, take drugs and drink. *I need your help.*

"It's like [if] you don't do that, you don't belong anywhere. I don't like that feeling. Most of my friends do all of that. My little brother, he's 7, listens to rock music.

"The reason I started was my mother and father broke up. My mom don't talk to me. My father never comes to see me. I have a twin brother. He takes drugs too.

"I thought if you could help me, you could tell me how to get away from it, then I could get him away from it.

"*Please help.*

"I say I hate my mother and father but I really don't. It's like if I don't have a mom and dad, I don't feel like living. It's so hard to get by in this world.

"I started listening to Motley Crue (Shout at the Devil) then I started listening to Iron Maiden.

"I know the Lord died for me *but the devil has me.* [At] times I feel like killing myself. But I don't want to go to <u>hell</u>.

*"Please help before something really happens.*

*"I need some kind of help. . . ."*

From a young woman in New York:

"Recently I read your article in 'Perhaps Today' magazine. I had a feeling of relief because there is a great need to talk to someone who has broken away from the occult.

"I work in a high school as a teacher's aide. We have physically handicapped and emotionally disturbed students.

"We picked up this new student . . . he was a Satanist and he knew I was a Christian. I became his target.

"This new student is deeply involved in the occult and is well read on the subject. There's drug involvement and he's really into rock music and the groups that lift up Satan. He has talked about mind control, guns, killing, all the time threatening us with death. . . . We have been told he was into animal sacrifices and the black mass.

"The thing that hurts the most is that I've always believed a saved Christian couldn't be bothered by any of this but I am. I'm of average intelligence and know some of this is nerves but I also know that young people today can become just that engrossed with evil. *Am I stupid, has this kid just convinced me he has the power to do these things, or does he?"*

From a woman in New York:

"When I was extremely young I was involved (because of my father) in a satanic cult. My father also sexually abused me, sold me to his friends and involved me in child pornography. I developed Multiple Personality Disorder (MPD) because of this . . .

"I tried Christian counselors but they said MPD was 'demons' and they tried to 'pray me through deliverance' and when I wasn't 'cured' they said I didn't *really* want to be free or God would have delivered/healed me of MPD . . .

"Please pray for me because I am tormented, thinking I have committed the unforgivable sin."

From a fifteen-year-old female in Minnesota:

"I was reading your tract on Satanism and at the end you mentioned about writing you. Well, I'm not into a cult, but I'm into Satanism. It all started like this: Well, I started using drugs when I was 11. I then was introduced to Satanism by some friends soon after. My Mom has always been a Christian. . . . So she knew what it was. I wore all black, listened to heavy metal, and had an altar in my bedroom.

"Well, after two years of that, I finally figured it out that Satanism wasn't getting me anywhere. I tried to leave it, but the demons scared me. . .

"A lot of my mom's friends are praying for me. But I think maybe they're (demons) inside of me too. *It scares me. I need help,* but my mom says all she can do is pray. *Can you help?"*

From a concerned parent in Pennsylvania:

"I have a 17 year old son that is really into Rock music and it about breaks my heart. I am a born again Christian and have always loved, sung, and played Gospel music on our radio or stereo. My son, is the opposite. He hates 'my music'. There is always a constant argument when we get into the car as to whose music we will listen to.

"I see the same pattern in our son as I read in your story. He is drawn to supernatural things but I have demanded no books on such (things) in our home. . . .

"I feel this Rock music is his downfall. In the last three years he has become hateful, angry, lazy, disrespectful, and nasty. He has let his homework drop to the point of failing 10th grade.

". . . We have gone to seek professional help but now he refuses to go at all. . . .

"We are at our wits end and are not sure what to do anymore or how to handle certain situations."

The information in this chapter should serve to illustrate the fact that participation in satanic or occult practices, regardless of how harmless they may appear initially, assuredly possesses the potential of extremely harmful, and often-times fatal, consequences or results.

Additionally, it is hoped that sufficient data has been offered to awaken the reader as to the tremendous need of believers who, recognizing their true position in the Lord, are willing to reach out to those who so desperately need their help, their advice, their love.

As we shall see as we proceed, offering such assistance to an individual who is involved in devil worship is generally not a simple undertaking. However, it is imperative that we comprehend the fact that such people truly can be reached and, in many cases, can ultimately be led to a genuine salvation experience with the Lord Jesus Christ.

# 4

# OCCULT SYMBOLS & WHAT THEY MEAN

Over the past several years I have received numerous letters from concerned parents and other individuals asking for an explanation of various symbols related to the occult. I have always stressed the fact that a true believer who has been washed in the blood of Jesus has nothing to fear from a kitchen mug with a zodiac sign on it or an item of jewelry that features a pentagram or other occult symbol. As Christians we have tremendous power and authority and are not to be bound by unfounded fears of such things (Luke 10:19; James 4:7; 1 John 4:4).

On the other hand however, this is not to imply that such signs and symbols should be ignored. As the Apostle Paul warned believers not to be ignorant of the enemy's devices, this chapter is included to inform concerned readers as to what the various symbols represent.

THE PENTAGRAM

The pentagram is perhaps one of the most popular occult symbols around today. It can be seen on rock album covers, books, and of course, necklaces and rings.

The pentagram is associated with witchcraft and usually denotes so-called pure magic or White Magic.

INVERTED PENTAGRAM

The inverted pentagram on the other hand is a symbol that generally represents evil or Black Magic. It is considered a powerful symbol and is used in satanic practices.

EMBLEM OF BAPHOMET

The inverted pentagram easily becomes the Emblem of Baphomet with the two upper points of the star representing horns, the two side points representing ears, and the bottom point of the star representing the chin. Baphomet is considered a demonic deity depicting Satan.

The Emblem of Baphomet appears on the front cover of Anton LaVey's Satanic Bible and is also popular with various rock musicians.

THE HEXAGRAM

The hexagram is generally considered to be the most powerful symbol in the occult arts. We use the root word "hex" when referring to a witch or Satanist casting a spell on someone.

It is believed that the Israelites began using this symbol during their captivity in Babylon. However, the Jewish Star of David should not be taken to represent occultism.

THAUMATURGIC TRIANGLE

The symbol depicted here is used for such magical practices as summoning demons or casting spells.

CRESCENT MOON & STAR

The Crescent Moon and Star is used to represent Diana the Queen or Goddess of Heaven, Moon, and Earth. This talisman may be worn as jewelry for protection against unwanted spirits.

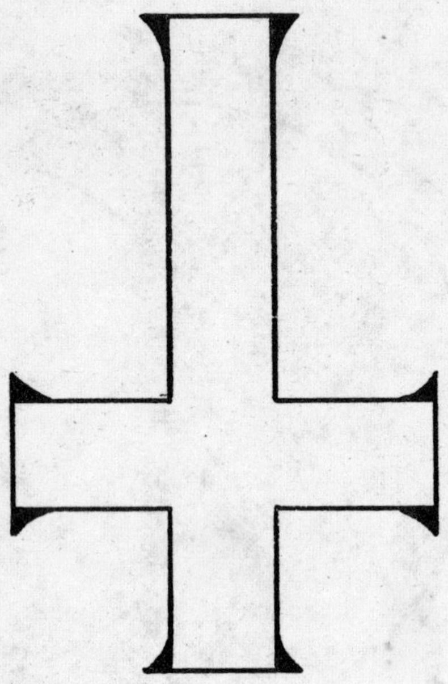

INVERTED CROSS

The inverted or Southern Cross symbolizes a rejection and mockery of the cross of Jesus Christ and the salvation that it stands for. The cross is turned upside down in order to let the Christianity drain from it.

Some Satanists actually have crosses tattooed on the soles of their feet so that they are constantly treading upon the cross of Jesus. Others may simply draw a cross on the bottoms of their shoes for the same purpose.

## PEACE SIGN

Some satanic cults take the inverted cross (described above) one step further in order to renounce the cross of Christ. An initiate is given a small ceramic cross, which he turns upside down in order to let the Christianity drain from it. He then grasps the inverted cross by the cross bars and breaks them downward (Fig. 1). Some people believe that this is what the "peace symbol" originally stood for.

However, as with the Star of David, there can be no doubt that countless individuals who display the peace symbol (Fig. 2) on their clothing or jewelry display it to promote peace and probably are not even aware of the occult significance of the emblem.

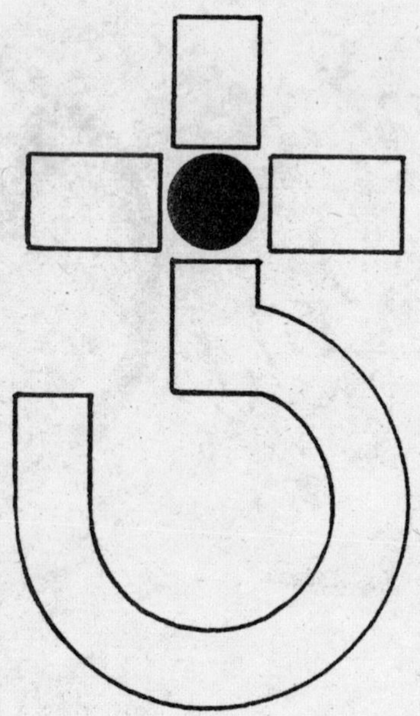

SATANIC CROSS

The Satanic Cross or Cross of Confusion is meant to question the message of the Christian faith and the effectiveness of the cross of Christ. The inverted question mark sarcastically asks, "Did Jesus *really* die for us?"

This symbol can be seen on the guitars and album covers of the rock group Blue Oyster Cult.

## CROSS OF LORRAINE

The Cross of Lorraine can be seen in the Satanic Bible as well as on rock album covers.

At the base of the cross we see the horizontal figure eight, which is the mathematical symbol for infinity. Many believe that the longer cross bar, which is *between* the cross bar on which Jesus was nailed and the infinity symbol below, represents the breaking of Christ's power (over sin/evil) for all time.

THE ANKH

The ankh is a symbol from ancient Egypt. It represents fertility and reincarnation. Many people who wear this symbol as a necklace seem to feel that it is simply a more fashionable or up-to-date version of the Christian cross. In truth, however, it most assuredly has nothing to do with the Christian faith.

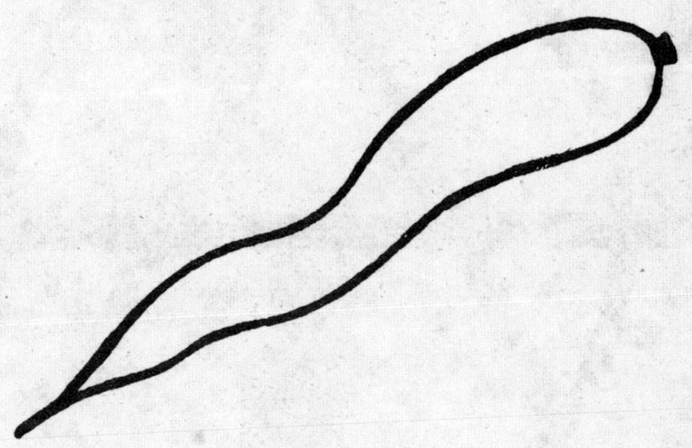

THE UNICORN HORN

Also known as the Italian Horn, Leprechaun's Staff, and Fairy Wand, this symbol signifies that the wearer is trusting Satan for his finances.

This symbol is extremely popular as a necklace but can also be seen resembling a large red pepper hanging from the rear view mirror of some cars.

ANARCHY SYMBOL

Often seen as graffiti spray-painted on buildings and bridges, the anarchy symbol is a bold declaration of rebellion and denial of authority.

The symbol, along with its clear meaning, is instrumental in the punk/new-wave music scene.

# 666

# FFF

## SIX HUNDRED, THREE SCORE & SIX

The 666 is used in reference to the Devil and/or the Antichrist. It is sometimes illustrated as *FFF* (*F* being the sixth letter of the alphabet).

The sign can be seen on countless rock music T-shirts, jackets, and album covers and at least one heavy metal band (Iron Maiden) actually has a song about it called "The Number of the Beast."

Unfortunately, it is obvious that those who so prominently display the 666 have no real understanding of just what the number means or what the man will be like who is represented by this number.

THE BLACK MASS

The symbols shown above are used to indicate a Black Mass.

THE ALL-SEEING EYE

Also called Udjat or The Eye of Horus, this symbol is referred to as the creator of men and things in the Egyptian Book of the Dead.

SATANIC LIGHTNING BOLT

This symbol, which was used for Adolph Hitler's notorious SS, can be seen on rock album covers and stage sets.

SWASTIKA

This ancient symbol is generally believed to represent the sun or other forces of nature. More recently, it has been used by Nazi and occult groups. When drawn in an anti-clockwise manner it represents flowing away from God.

DUNG BEETLE

The Egyptian dung beetle, or scarab, is a symbol of reincarnation. As with other Egyptian symbols, the scarab can be found on some rock album covers.

# NATAS

# REDRUM

## BACKWARD WRITING

Satanists frequently write words backwards both as a mockery of the proper way of doing things as well as to confuse the average layman. The words above, *NATAS,* which is *SATAN* spelled backwards, and *REDRUM,* which is *MURDER* spelled backwards, are two of the most popular words among teen-agers and dabblers. Such words are often seen on school notebooks and as graffiti on buildings and bridges.

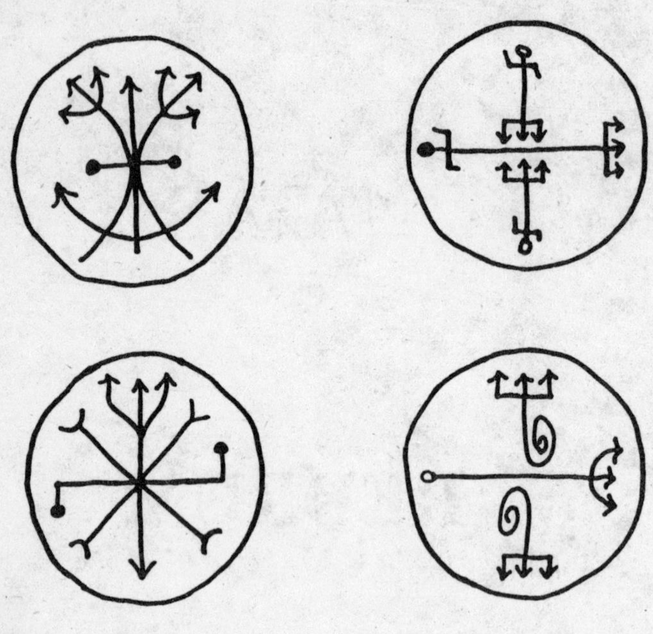

## VODOUN

More detailed and intricate symbols, such as those illustrated above, are usually an indication of some type of vodoun (voodoo) activity as opposed to witchcraft or Satanism. Such signs are usually not drawn by youngsters or dabblers and are generally drawn on the ground. Any such drawings found on one's property, particularly at the front door, should be reported to proper authorities immediately. Nothing in the vicinity should be touched or moved and, if possible, photographs should be taken of the symbol(s).

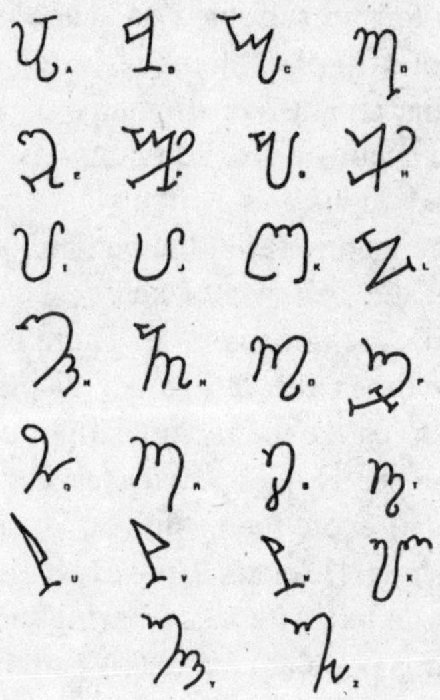

## WITCHES ALPHABET

The figures illustrated here are referred to as the "Witches Alphabet." Although many different covens, sects, and circles have their own private alphabets to ensure privacy, the one illustrated above is the most common among teen-agers and dabblers.

As a teen-age Satanist myself, I once wrote threatening letters to enemies in the above style. Although the addressee could neither read nor understand such notes, it generally served the purpose of planting fear in his/her heart.

A ghoulish drawing I was given while lecturing in the Atlantic Provinces (Canada), drawn by a fourteen-year-old boy, featured several of the above "letters" across the top of the page.

* * * * * * * *

It should be understood that this chapter has considered only the most popular occult symbols, which one is most likely to find scribbled on school notebooks, spray-painted as graffiti or as items of jewelry. This analysis is by no means exhaustive as many of the various sects, covens, and occult-related religions have hundreds of their own detailed signs and symbols.

As was mentioned at the beginning of this chapter, I would urge the believer to keep a cool head whenever such symbols are encountered. There is nothing to fear.

Many times the individual displaying the symbol doesn't even realize the relationship it may have to occult practices. I recently questioned a teen-age boy at a Toronto shopping mall about the upside down cross he was wearing as an earring. He claimed to have no interest in Satanism whatsoever and said he was wearing the ear piece simply because it was popular. While this certainly does not mean that I condone the wearing of inverted crosses or other pieces of occult jewelry, it does support the fact that people wearing such items should not be immediately labelled as bloodthirsty, vicious, ritual killers.

It is far more sensible to keep a cool, logical attitude when considering occult signs and symbols rather than allowing fear or paranoia to distort the facts.

# 5

# STRICTLY FOR PARENTS

No one is in a better position to help kids avoid involvement with Satanism than parents. At first consideration this statement may seem to place an unfair burden of responsibility on the mothers and fathers of teen-agers today. But quite frankly, it is a burden that men and women should be prepared to assume when they choose to have children.

Let's put it another way. Generally speaking it is the responsibility of the parents to make sure their children attend school. It is the responsibility of the parents to make sure their children are fed and well cared for. It is the responsibility of the parents to teach their children those things that are fundamentally acceptable and proper and to discourage those things that are wrong or illegal.

And it is also the responsibility of the parents to teach children that involvement with the occult/Satanism, like involvement with drugs or alcohol, is potentially dangerous and can result in extremely unpleasant repercussions.

A police officer provides some similar insights: "Kids who get in trouble around here, the one thing they'd have in common is their home background. Single parents, or maybe both parents are working. *Too busy for any real family life* . . . If you ask me about the one thing every kid should have, it wouldn't be money. It wouldn't even be an education. It would be a good, solid, old-fashioned family.

"You see," the policeman continued, "we have all these programs for kids nowadays. We have anti-drug programs and programs against teenage pregnancy. We go into schools and advertise on TV to tell young people about drinking or safe sex. We have youth bureaus and social workers. We have career counselling and driver training and student loans.

"We have a fancy program for just about every problem a kid could possibly have. Yet kids have more problems with pregnancy or with drugs or with dropping out than they've ever had back in the old days before we came up with any of these programs. *The only thing we don't have for kids anymore is a strong family.* Parents who stick together, who set the rules and see that the kids obey them. . . . Maybe most children don't need it so badly. . . . They'll grow up to be pretty decent people anyway. But some do, and if they don't get it at home, I don't know where else they can get it. I don't think they'll get it in juvenile court or in jail."[1]

A distinction should be made at this juncture. It should be noted that responsibility and fault are two entirely different things. As we have mentioned, it is surely the parents' obligation and duty to do all within their means to raise their children in positive, morally balanced homes. But this in no way is meant to imply that it is always the *fault* of the parents when a young person becomes involved in Satanism.

Many times and for various reasons, despite the best efforts on the part of the parents, teen-agers choose to involve themselves with things they know they should not become involved with—things like Satanism. Unfortunately, many non-Christian parents (not to mention many Christian parents) tend to feel that the issue of Satanism among our young people is nothing more than a "religious issue" that doesn't concern them or their children. In many cases the paranoid extremes of believers over the years have led to this apathetic condition.

But it is necessary to comprehend the consequential fact that satanic involvement knows no boundaries. Kids from every walk of life and every social level are delving into devil worship in droves. The problem of Satanism among our youth is not merely a religious issue. It is nothing less than a social issue that needs to be dealt with expediently.

Fortunately there exists several warning signs, which parents can watch for that might indicate an unhealthy interest in the occult or Satanism.

While evidence of these signs cannot be considered as positive proof that your child is dabbling in the black arts, and one or two signs should not give rise to alarm, if you should notice several of the following signs or symptoms displayed by your child, it may be time to take the matter seriously.

## WARNING SIGNS OF POSSIBLE OCCULT INTEREST OR INVOLVEMENT

1. An obsession with or addiction to heavy metal rock-and-roll music. Particularly those bands that blatantly promote Satanism through occult symbols on album covers or references to Satan, demons, suicide, or death in their lyrics.

2. Interest in occult or satanic paraphernalia (e.g., skulls, black-handled knives, chalices, black candles, robes, etc.).

3. Interest in satanic literature (e.g., *The Satanic Bible*, *Necronomicon*, etc.).

4. Obsession with or addiction to horror movies that tend to glorify Satan, sacrifices, rituals, death, etc.

5. Preoccupation with Ouija boards, tarot cards, astral projection, etc.

6. Obsession with or addiction to fantasy role playing games such as Dungeons and Dragons, Chivalry and Sorcery, etc.

7. Inclination to write poetry, song lyrics or letters about suicide, blood, death, or Satan.

8. References to thoughts of suicide either written (as in #7 above) or spoken.

9. Inclination to draw occult or satanic symbols on notebooks, clothing, or other possessions.

10. Frequent wearing of black clothing and/or jewelry that incorporates occult or satanic symbols.

11. Sudden uncharacteristic displays of anger or aggression.

12. Abrupt drop in grades at school.

13. Extra-curricular activities, sports, hobbies, etc., are avoided.

14. Self-mutilation (i.e., occult or Satanic symbols drawn or carved on skin, home-made tattoos).

15. Exchange of large group of friends for a smaller, more select group.

Now that we know what signs to look for, which may indicate that our teen-ager is dabbling in the occult, we are immediately faced with the obvious question, "What can we do about it?" This is where we talk about the hard part. It's a difficult topic, all too often avoided, called "work." Yes, it is a four-letter-word. But an important word nevertheless.

We live in a very fast-paced society today. Everything has to be done yesterday and nothing can wait for tomorrow. Many families spend too little time together because each member of the family is caught up in the trend of constantly doing something. Dad may be a member of the bowling league or a union representative with meetings to attend. He may be the kind of man who likes to go out to the local pub three or four nights a week just to kick back with the guys and down a few beers to relax after a hard day at work. Or he may even be overly involved with church.

Perhaps he is a deacon or maybe he just likes to take care of things at the church like mowing the lawn or weeding the flower garden out front. Mom may love her bingo games three or four nights a week or maybe she is taking a microwave cooking class at the local night school. Or she may find that she is always having to bring her work home with her from the office just to keep from falling behind. Daughter is off at the library "studying" with friends, down at the mall shopping or maybe out on a date while Son is playing basketball, football, or hockey.

So often the parents don't have any idea where their kids are at any given moment or, on the other side of the coin, the kids may not be able to find an opening in their parents' busy schedules to talk to them about problems they are facing or questions they might have.

As we saw earlier, this problem alone is a major reason why kids get involved in Satanism. Sadly, it is sometimes the only way they can think of to effectively get the attention of Mom and Dad.

"The kids out there worshiping Satan, holding ceremonies and writing graffiti on the walls probably aren't really worshiping Satan. I think, for the most part, they're probably feeling unloved by their parents, or just feeling lonely and bored."[2]

Jerry Johnston points out that teen-agers commit suicide everyday because "they think that there's nobody there, that nobody cares."[3]

I believe the first step in correcting the above situation is for each family member, particularly Mom and Dad who are expected to play the part of role models, to commit themselves to spending more time with the other members of the family. This can often be as simple as planning a weekly evening out at a local restaurant.

All too often parents are willing to let their kids go off on their own rather than joining the family, not realizing that their son or daughter may truly want to be included in the family's plans. This situation was typified for me recently by a family I know personally. A nineteen-year-old girl who lives with her parents was left at home while her mother and father spent a week in Florida. When they returned home the daughter, we'll call her

Sandy, mentioned that she was a little hurt and disappointed that she had not been invited to go along.

Mom and Dad were surprised and sincerely sorry. It's important to understand that they didn't intend to offend their daughter. They simply assumed that she would prefer to stay home, have the house to herself and go ahead with any plans she may have had rather than spending a week with her parents. The key to this problem is that they *assumed* rather than asked.

One cannot help but wonder how often this occurs in homes throughout the U.S. and Canada. How often do parents just presume that their kids don't want to be included in their plans when in reality, nothing would make him/her happier.

It must also be stated that the practice of inviting and lovingly encouraging children to be involved with various family activities should be maintained even when, or better still, especially when the child involved is not particularly interested in the idea.

In other words, if you develop the practice of going out for pizza every Wednesday evening together as a family but your sixteen-year-old son routinely declines the invitation, *this should not cause you to stop letting him know he is welcome to join you whenever he would like.*

Frequently I hear from parents who have become frustrated because they have attempted to communicate better with their teen-agers but the kids don't seem to want any part of it. But we shouldn't expect such things to happen overnight. Anything and everything you read about in this book requires work and commitment. There's no avoiding that truth. But after all, aren't your kids worth the effort?

The adult, whether a parent or not, must understand that the peer pressures teen-agers face today are tremendously difficult to handle. Try to imagine a tough-looking seventeen-year-old who wears black leather, torn blue jeans, and has a pierced ear. The kids he hangs around with consider him to be one of them. He's tough, he's smooth, he's cool.

Now is it possible for us to even begin to comprehend just how hard it would be for such a kid to suddenly leave his friends once or twice a week and spend time with his family? His status among his peers would go right down the drain. He'd be considered a "wimp," a "Momma's boy," or worse.

This is precisely why we as adults desperately need to try harder to better understand what the kids of today are up against. As we begin to grasp what life is like for them we will also begin to see how unrealistic many of our expectations really are.

As I travel around the country lecturing on the subject of Satanism or during television and radio interviews, I strongly encourage parents to take the time to familiarize themselves with the world *as the younger generation perceives it.* I believe this advice is paramount for all parents regardless of their religious or spiritual views. To be honest, what I am referring to is really quite simple, and as far as I'm concerned, there is not one valid reason for a parent to refute it.

**Getting to Know Kids (Especially Your Own!)**

I never fail to notice a few shocked expressions on adult faces whenever I share the following advice at meetings and seminars. Certainly some of the suggestions that follow may be considered unconventional or even extreme. However, I believe that any parent should be more than willing to exercise such relatively simple measures when the very lives of their children may depend on them.

The first step toward better understanding your kids as well as better understanding why they say and do the things they do, is to familiarize yourself with what they are feeding themselves. And I don't mean food. The Word of God tells us that the information and stimulation we expose ourselves to basically shapes and molds us into what we become (Matt. 12:34; Phil. 4:8; etc.). In other words, if we constantly take in negative data, through various non-Christian or non-moral channels such as movies, novels, or music, we will begin to live our lives and shape our values based upon the negative influences we are allowing into our heart.

A recent article in a major Toronto newspaper verifies this fact:

"Satanic Junk 'A Threat to Kids'"—"Teenagers are being saturated by satanic propaganda, a cult expert told Toronto high school students yesterday.

"Satanic and violent images are used increasingly in popular books, music, videos and movies, said Robert Tucker, executive director of the Council On Mind Abuse.

"The philosophy behind those images often encourages 'mental health pollution'—hostility, intolerance and emotional indifference, Tucker said. . . . 'You are being exposed to a fairly intensive propaganda campaign in which you are being desensitized.'

"He (Tucker) urged students to question movies that almost glorify killing, like 'Nightmare on Elm Street,' and heavy-metal videos and lyrics that 'celebrate' satanic acts of murder, dismemberment, suicide and degradation of women."[4]

It is for this reason that I strongly encourage parents to acquaint themselves with the various sources of information their children are feeding upon. One of the easiest ways to begin a project such as this is to go through your child's record or tape collection. Many of the albums have song lyrics printed on the album jacket or include a lyric sheet inside the album jacket or cassette case.

The albums that do not include lyric sheets can still be scrutinized simply by examining the artwork on the jacket, which frequently displays vulgar or sexual innuendos or blatant satanic symbols. Of course, a simple reading of the song titles can also reveal the general message that particular bands are delivering.

An important point to stress here is that I am in no

way suggesting that a parent sneak through their son's or daughter's belongings without politely and casually mentioning their desire to do so to the child involved. Such an invasion of privacy has the potential to cause quite a lot of damage to the relationship between you and your kids. Besides, if handled correctly, the mere fact that you are taking an interest in your child might cause him or her to realize that you really do care!

If your child is a little older and takes his privacy that much more seriously, it may be a better idea to simply spend ten or fifteen minutes browsing through the albums at the record store the next time you're out shopping. This is also an excellent way for concerned adults, youth workers, or pastors who may not have children of their own to familiarize themselves with the most powerful of all influences upon kids today.

Eric Barger discusses this in his book, *From Rock to Rock*. "Parents: Take an active part in what your children and teens listen to (and watch). It may not be an enjoyable thing to do but DO IT! Sit down and listen with them. Check out the radio stations to which they listen and the T.V. and videos they may choose to view. Be watchful of how the music they hear (and visuals they see) affects their attitude. Stay informed! Read the lyrics on the album jackets. Maybe even take the big leap and read up on the latest rock stars and what they are up to. You can find a number of monthly magazines on rock music at your local convenience store.

"Providing an alternative is important. Do not expect the 15-year-old boy who loves Guns N' Roses to immediately crave Sandi Patti, but a musical substitute is needed. Thank the Lord there are good God-centered alternatives."[5]

"Parents need to become familiar with their children's favorite music. They should not be put off by the unusual clothing or hair styles of the entertainers. Every generation rebels against the previous, though most adults will not admit they may have defied their own parents. We should listen to the lyrics of songs and attend the concerts to see what is taking place. Then we should place appropriate restrictions, not on lifestyle but on inappropriate and unhealthy actions. We can focus on the worst and ignore the rest or develop an uneasy truce."[6]

Barger brings out an excellent concept, which I always share with the audience during lectures and seminars. The simple and inexpensive idea of picking up two or three issues of the various rock magazines every once in a while is perhaps the easiest and quickest way in which to find out just what is happening in the rock music industry today.

Since there are several different music magazines on the newsstands each month, I would suggest that you obtain three or four different titles so that you can get a fairly good overview of the rock music scene.

There is little doubt that you will find some of these publications to be blatantly offensive and perverse. You might be repulsed by what the rock idols themselves have to say in interviews. The photographs might disgust or even nauseate you. *But that could be just what parents need in order to wake-up.*

A bottom-line approach to the situation is to simply listen to some of the albums or tapes yourself. Pay close attention to what is said. You may want to take notes and keep a list of how often references are made to Satan, the occult, drugs, etc., thereby equipping yourself to have a knowledgeable, rational conversation with your child as to why you are uncomfortable with such music in your home.

The same can be done with rock music videos that are shown twenty-four hours a day on some cable television networks. You may prefer to rent videos of your child's favorite bands at your local video store. As you watch, remember to take notes. After you have gathered enough evidence to support your case, you may wish to view the video *with* your child, pausing the tape from time to time to discuss the negative aspects of it.

Many parents would be surprised at how some young people will tend to agree with them if actual facts are presented in a calm and mature manner. Oftentimes it is simply a matter of the child being previously unaware of the various problems you have noticed in the music/videos.

My last suggestion in this particular area is the one that generally raises the most eyebrows when I mention it at my seminars. . . . Why not go to a rock concert with your kid! Now before you toss this book aside in disgust, please allow me to explain myself.

Time and time again I meet parents, including Christian parents, who think nothing of allowing their children to attend live performances by some of the most offensive of the rock-and-roll performers. In fact, it is not uncommon to see kids as young as nine or ten-years-old at some shows!

My point is simply this: If you see no harm in allowing your young person to participate in such activities, why not go along and find out for yourself what rock concerts are really like? I can hear many of my readers at this point. "I hate that loud rock stuff. I'd never go to a concert and have to listen to it!" Again I must stress that none of these suggestions will be particularly enjoyable for the majority of adults. But aren't your kids worth it?

Many parents are shocked and disgusted to learn that some of the concerts they have unwittingly allowed their kids to attend sometimes end with the performers inviting any interested parties to come to the stage to accept Satan as their lord and saviour!

### What About Record Burning?

Many Christian adults are disappointed when I point out that I do not advocate or condone the burning of rock albums. Certainly many preachers and evangelists have encouraged and promoted the concept over the years, but many of us are beginning to look back and realize that although the act itself usually generates a lot of media attention (usually making Christians look ridiculous), it frequently fails to help the kids in the long run.

My own experience serves as an illustration. After being involved in the occult and Satanism as a teen-ager and being quite literally addicted to heavy metal rock music, I accepted the Lord Jesus as my Saviour (see chapter 1).

In my desire to please the Lord and serve Him, I hastily did what several believers directed me to do—I smashed hundreds of dollars worth of rock-and-roll albums. And before too long, I went out and bought brand new copies of the same albums I had smashed.

Again referring to Barger we read, "Warning—Warning! If you force your teen to destroy his or her records you may win the battle but lose the war. Though the Word tells us to guide and direct their paths, ultimately *they have to make the choice* to get rid of the junk. If you do it, I guarantee the kids will get it back somehow and may even spend more of God's money on the same garbage again. For many young people (and some adults too), severing with the secular music scene may be the hardest thing they have ever done. To make this tremendously tough decision they need (1) information, (2) understanding, and (3) prayer"(italics mine).[7]

A situation I encountered several years ago might help to shed some light on this area. I had the pleasure of holding in-home Bible studies a few years ago. One night we were pleased to have a young unwed mother join us for the class. This young woman, let's call her "Denise," began to attend the studies on a regular basis, and we were thrilled to watch how the Lord was working with her. Before long she accepted Jesus as her Saviour.

During one of our subsequent studies, a Christian man and his wife who joined us occasionally invited this new believer to their home for lunch the following day. Over the next few weeks Denise was absent from the studies and since none of us had heard from her, we decided to get in touch just to let her know that we missed her and were anxious to have her join us again. We were dumbfounded by what she told us when we met with her.

Apparently the couple who had invited Denise to have lunch with them didn't hesitate to serve her up as the main course! She told us that she was "raked over the coals" during her entire visit. She was lectured on how wrong it was for her to be living with a man who was not her husband, how she simply had to begin attending church services every week, how she couldn't possibly be a real Christian until she stopped smoking cigarettes, and on and on it went.

Now let me hasten to point out that I believe it is wrong for a couple to live together without the benefit of marriage. Nor do I feel that people, Christian or otherwise, should smoke. And yes, church attendance is important.

The problem though, is that Denise was a brand new believer. She was neither prepared nor willing to make such immediate changes in her life. As a matter of fact, she could no more make such drastic changes "overnight" than the average alcoholic can simply stop drinking or the individual who has chain-smoked for thirty years can quit "cold turkey." *It just isn't that easy.*

Denise never did come back to the Bible studies. All because some "holier-than-thou" Christians felt that they had to take it upon themselves to finish the work that Christ had started in this young woman's life. When will we begin to allow the Lord to do what only He can do? (Phil. 1:6)

It cannot be denied that in a tremendously large number of instances a teen-ager's love and desire for rock-and-roll music is nothing less than an obsession or addiction. This is where adults in general, and parents in particular, need to understand the difficult and confusing position they put their children in when they demand that he or she simply stop listening to rock music.

I have found that in an overwhelming majority of cases the kids are neither pleased nor amused when they are brought to the realization that they are virtual slaves to music.

Again and again when I offer the challenge for young people to completely stop listening to rock music for three straight days, I am immediately greeted by shouts of, "I can't" or "That's not possible." Interestingly however, when I ask the kids if that fact bothers them, the response is almost always a resounding "YES"! (I have only received a "no" response one time as of this writing.)

However, as this chapter is addressed primarily to parents, I would like to hereby challenge you to partake in a similar project just to help you to better understand how difficult it really is.

In order to help you to sympathize with your kids, who may be having a terrible struggle with their addiction to music, I encourage you, the parents, to do the following for a minimum of three consecutive days.

1. Turn off the television. This means no sports, no news, and no soap operas. (They can be addicting too!)

2. Turn off your records or your favorite radio station. You'll quickly see just how tough it is to break a habit (again, don't even tune in to the newscasts).

3. Put away the romance novels and detective magazines.

**A Few More Suggestions. . . .**

**Don't try to be a kid!** Don't be afraid to act your age. Whether they readily admit it or not, kids want their parents to be someone they can look up to and respect. It's O.K. to be "with it," in fact it's imperative, but don't start wearing skin-tight jeans and leather jackets with safety pins!

**Don't throw your parental authority around.** That usually doesn't solve anything. Instead of yelling and threatening, try attacking the problem slowly and gradually. Learn to *talk* with your kids and remember to *listen* when they talk to you.

**Stay in touch with your kid.** Don't hesitate to make

appointments with school teachers, principals, or guidance counsellors. After all, they're your children and you have every right to keep up with what's happening with them.

**Avoid double standards!** This is important! Don't read books or watch movies that deal with the occult or Satanism or listen to any of the questionable country and western music if you've been on your kid's case about what he/she listens to and watches! People who live in glass houses . . .

**Be informed.** Don't always leave things to the "experts." Read books, talk to counsellors, pastors or police officers. Keep yourself abreast of what is happening with young people today.

**Be aware of any traumatic experience your child might go through** (e.g., death of a friend or family member, divorce of parents, trouble with the law, etc.). Such occurrences can often open the door to cult or occult involvement as the young person searches for answers.

**Take note of radical changes in mood, attitude, or behavior.** If your child suddenly stops eating meat because he believes it is healthier to be a vegetarian that's one thing. But if he stops eating meat because he believes it is sacred or holy, you need to find out where these ideas are coming from. Also, if your normally kind, polite, considerate child suddenly becomes irritable and miserable, you need to keep your eye on him.

**Do not dismiss symptoms as nothing more than a "fad"!** Many parents who have done so are now dead and buried or their child is in serious legal trouble or worse. Sure, your kid may just be experiencing normal teen-age rebellion. But then again, there may be more to it than that, and based on recent cases of teen-age satanic involvement, murder, and suicide, you really can't afford to take that chance.

**Get professional help!** If you have reason to believe that your child is actively involved in anything potentially dangerous or life-threatening, do not hesitate to seek professional assistance. Many hospitals and police departments are now specially trained to help families in such situations.

* * * * * * *

*" . . . there's gonna come a time if your child is involved in the occult—there's gonna be a time your child reaches out and asks for help. Maybe just one time. And if you're not there to see what's going on, if you're not there when that child reaches out, he might never do it again. I reached out one time—but there was nobody there for me."*[8]

Sean Sellers

*(Sean Sellers is presently awaiting execution by lethal injection for sacrificing three people, including his parents, to Satan.)*

# 6

# WHY DON'T KIDS LIKE CHURCH?

*The mission of the Church today seems to be focused on winning souls. People go into the streets, pass out tracts, have huge evangelistic meetings, lead thousands to the Lord . . . and then abandon them. We're like an army of loggers running through the forest chopping down trees and leaving them to rot on the ground . . .*

Sean Sellers[1]

* * * * * * *

Although this chapter is sure to draw sighs of disapproval and disagreement from many readers, there is much that truly needs to be said about how the Christian Church today is failing to reach out to young people. Perhaps a better way to phrase the question "Why don't kids like church?" would simply be "Why should they?"

As mentioned in the opening chapter, my own childhood experiences with a mainline protestant church were certainly less than fulfilling or enriching. The particular church I attended with my parents had absolutely nothing to offer a young, energetic child. The pastor was generally quite lifeless and constantly spoke in a monotone voice. The songs we sang were always the slowest, driest hymns in the song book and the sermons were based on topics that held no relevance to young people (e.g., parenting, grand-parenting, finances, etc.).

Of course we heard plenty about the birth of a little

baby named Jesus around the Christmas holidays and about how the pitiful, scrawny man was cruelly beaten and crucified.

But it was never explained to me that this little baby, who was born in a dirty stable, was actually God Himself. I was never told that through His death He actually conquered death, hell and the grave and defeated the devil. No one in my family had any idea that Jesus is coming back one day to finally and triumphantly put an end to the sorrow and suffering of mankind.

Naturally the first thing on the minds of many readers is that I probably would have enjoyed Sunday school more than the actual Sunday morning sermons. Well, let me tell you about Sunday school. I remember one Sunday in particular when the teachers rounded up all of us and took us for a nice long walk on the church property. Another time we made cute pictures with colored paper and crayons. Quite often we would play various games.

Basically, Sunday school was the same as primary school. The only obvious difference was that we sang some cute Christian songs at the beginning of each Sunday school session and joined together for prayer before leaving.

Now please understand, I am not saying that all churches or all Sunday school classes are conducted in this manner. I thank God that there are many fine Sunday school teachers who are doing an exemplary job of teaching our little ones about the Lord and His Word. Unfortunately, such teachers are the exception rather than the rule.

Neither do I wish to come across as a spoiled child who wouldn't have found anything nice to say about church if his life depended on it. The sad fact is that as I travel throughout the United States and Canada and talk with teen-agers, and they all have the same story to tell. They don't go to church because, for the most part, it is dead, boring, and dull.

In case you haven't yet figured it out, the problem I

am referring to here is not so much what the Church is doing *but what it is not doing.*

Ted Schwarz and Duane Empey, authors of the book *Satanism*, provide insight into this problem.

"Rabouin (a former Satanist) delighted in the manipulation of others. He understood why people sought the church, and he understood what took them from it. He spoke of people seeking guidance but being stopped by the church secretary with such lines about the priest as 'he plays golf every Wednesday afternoon. He needs his rest, poor dear; he works so hard. I just make it a policy of not letting anything be scheduled that would interrupt his game. Let me schedule you for some other time, some other day.'

"Rabouin discovered through his observations that although the priests were hard-working, they seemed to be overprotective of their own time. He decided to make himself the equivalent of a convenience food store, opening his home to those seeking solace twenty-four hours a day. Whenever someone came or called, he or she was not turned away. 'They asked for help and they went away filled. Whatever their need, whether it was to have someone listen to them or to request a spell, I satisfied them. They would complain about their ministers, their priests. *I gave them what the clergy was not providing. And who do you think appeared to be the most spiritual? The churches were providing me with souls because they were not doing their job . . .*'

"Although some Satanists are violent and perverted, most are not. The majority who have been interviewed are searching souls who feel themselves betrayed by the church as they know it" (italics mine).[2]

This point is later reiterated, "When Christianity rejects troubled people, they sometimes turn not only to cults but also to Satanism.

"In some instances, the church may reject its own by not following through on its beliefs. For example, it is one thing to oppose abortion; it is another to provide the long-term emotional support needed by pregnant teens. . . . *Satanism on its own might not be on the rise, but the Church by its practices is giving it many willing victims*" (italics mine).[3]

In many cases the pastors, youth workers, and parents are simply failing to comprehend the fact that their young people are individual human beings with their own particular likes and dislikes. So many parents take it for granted that their children will enjoy and benefit from the church they attend just because they (the parents) have been members for several years.

Unfortunately, just because Mr. and Mrs. Smith enjoy attending the church down the street doesn't necessarily mean that their thirteen-year-old daughter or their seventeen-year-old son are as comfortable with the idea.

Maybe, just maybe, the kids would actually look forward to Sundays if they were allowed to go the church two blocks over—the one with the dynamic youth pastor who actually knows the names of the popular contemporary Christian musicians and sometimes even leaves his house without a tie! But more about this later.

We need to become more sensitive to the needs of young people today. Many of the old lines no longer ring true and most of the old logic just doesn't work anymore. Needless to say, this doesn't mean that the Lord or the Gospel has changed, it simply means that we—the believers—have become locked into an antediluvian outlook, which is preventing us from relating to the kids of the nineties.

The outdated reasoning that says, "If it was good enough for my father and it was good enough for me, it's good enough for my boy" no longer applies. Teen-agers today are facing more pressures, stronger intimidation, and greater temptation to reject the Lord than any of us ever would have dreamed possible even a decade ago.

Perhaps some of my readers can remember back to

what it meant to be "cool" during their childhood days. Back then a young guy was considered cool if he had the courage to smoke a cigarette behind the barn or steal a girlie magazine from his father's sock drawer.

Not too long ago, all it took to be cool was long hair and a loud motorcycle. Of course, to really be part of the "in crowd" you had to smoke a joint every now and then and spice up your vocabulary with the "*F* word."

But kids today are in a far more desperate position. The desire to be noticed is still there along with the yearning to be rebellious. The problem, however, is that it is becoming harder and harder for the teens to effectively shock the adults. We've been exposed to so much over the past quarter of a century or so that we've naturally toughened our skin. This has made it necessary for those who wish to shock us to resort to the most vile, heinous, vulgar acts they can dream up.

"An FBI behavioral sciences expert believes some of the rising interest (in Satanism) stems from a simple itch to ride the edge of social convention. 'People want to toy with forbidden things. They're kind of like moths flying around a damn flame just to see how close they can get without getting burned. And you must consider how little is forbidden today', said the agent, assigned to the FBI training academy at Quantico, Va. 'We accept things now that would've been unheard of 20 years ago. That's one reason why what's attractive is so much more extraordinarily evil.'"[4]

Something as relatively minor as swearing at a school teacher or spitting on a police officer might be enough to traumatize our dear old grandmothers, but those who find themselves surrounded by such activities on a frequent basis (e.g., school teachers, social workers, guidance counsellors) have necessarily hardened themselves to it and the kids know it.

The average seventeen-year-old high school student with a sprinkling of rebelliousness notices this. Ten years ago he may have done something as comparatively harmless as breaking a window in order to get attention. But now he finds he may have to desecrate cemeteries, mutilate neighborhood pets, or carve up his own flesh in order to achieve the same results.

In his book, *Witches, Pagans, & Magic in the New Age*, Kevin Marron explains the necessity of understanding just what it is that Satanists are rejecting and why they are rejecting it. Marron provides a thought-provoking challenge, which in effect forms the basis of this chapter.

Patti Lalonde, co-publisher of *The Christian World Report*, relates an eye-opening experience she and her husband shared: "A few months ago my husband spoke at one such church near our hometown. He spoke about the New Age Movement and the deceptive dangers of meditation, trance channelling and so forth. At the end of the session, Peter gave a question and answer period. A teenage boy stood up and asked, 'Don't you think that one of the reasons so many young people are trying this stuff is because they are looking for something real? And they're sick and tired of parents and adults claiming to be spiritual Christians, but by their actions you know they haven't got a thing?' Talk about being hit with spiritual reality!

"In their desire to find something to fill the spiritual void; the emptiness that can only be filled by Christ, many young people turn to Satanism.

*"If we, the church, do not possess the reality we claim, the world will look elsewhere for it.* And make no mistake, Satan is working overtime to offer counterfeit after counterfeit."[6]

We have said that young people today are basically bored with the routine of living in the 1990s. They are reaching out to Satanism and the occult in order to find a new, exciting pastime, hobby, or religion.

Add to this boredom the fact that many families today consist of fathers and mothers who are both employed outside the home and we arrive at the second major factor of many teen-agers' involvement in Satanism—their desire to be noticed. Let me hasten to add that it is not my intention to cast blame or condemnation on two-income families. Indeed, many families couldn't possibly survive today's economy with a single income. My point is simply that, for the most part, our young people are being ignored or neglected and many are turning to Satanism for no other reason than to remind their parents that they're still around.

We have also pointed out that in many cases, "Satanism" may be nothing more than the expression of common teen-age rebellion that every generation seems to experience. Whether it be rebellion against society, rebellion against authority, or simply rebellion against parental rules, such insubordination and defiance has characterized adolescence for countless years.

While keeping all of these components in mind, it is the purpose of this chapter to analyze, first of all, the role the Church plays, if any, in causing young people to seek out alternative and sometimes dangerous affiliations and, secondly, to consider possible preventative or corrective steps, which the Church might take to reverse this unhealthy process.

Perhaps one of the most important considerations in this area is that which is expressed in the book, *The Edge of Evil*. "What the children are really rebelling against is that we do not give children a religion of experience in our culture. We only give them a religion of thought and of social responsibility."[7]

This information becomes convincingly puissant when one ruminates the differences between several other religions as they compare to Christianity. Consider for example a prominent derivative of the vodoun religion, Santaria or its more sinister counterpart, Palo Mayombe. The observance of these religious beliefs includes multifarious rituals and ceremonies combining fanciful belief structures and colorful fetishes. Candles, bonfires, magic potions, detailed chants, amulets, ceremonial dances, and animal sacrifices are often indispensable ingredients in the practice of the vodoun religion.

The diverse beliefs and the corresponding ceremonies of the various North American Indian tribes also include exciting and stimulating participation of its adherents. Detailed costumes made up of incredibly ornate bead work and brilliantly colored feathers along with the pelts, teeth and claws of assorted wild animals such as the wolf or buffalo are worn by the participants.

High-ranking elders of the tribe wear magnificently decorative headdresses made up of hundreds of feathers. The dances they perform are certainly not the unplanned or awkward displays that are so often misrepresented by the movie industry. Rather, each dance, each ceremony is carefully and painstakingly choreographed and handed down from generation to generation.

We might also mention the aboriginal tribes of the Australian outback. These hearty people also take their religious beliefs very seriously. Their rituals may consist of strenuous dancing and colorful patterns painted directly on their flesh. In each of the above cases, the particular ceremony might last for several hours or even several days!

Perhaps a good example, which is closer to home, would be the Jewish religion. The Jews celebrate several different festivals and holy days throughout the year with names like The Festival of Freedom (Passover), Feast of Firstfruits (Easter), New Year's Day (Rosh Hashanah), Feast of Tabernacles (Succoth) and Feast of Lights (Hanukkah). The various holidays and celebrations include intricate and deeply meaningful traditions, rituals, and customs as well as special foods and distinctive articles of clothing.

Now consider the average North American church service. Parishioners are herded into a stuffy, confined "church" building and seated on hard wooden benches. Each one, regardless of age or sex, is dressed in his or her most attractive (and least comfortable!) Sunday clothes. An air of deep, almost catatonic reverence is expected from all.

The minister greets his congregation from the pulpit and directs them to open their hymn books to the particular song he has chosen for the opening hymn. More often than not it is a beautiful, meaningful number but this fact is generally overlooked by the majority who cannot get past the dry and monotonous tempo or the "King James English" of it.

Next comes the announcements. This is perhaps the portion of our weekly religious service that has less to do with our actual religious beliefs or the practice of them than any other aspect of the service. We hear about the need for volunteers to cut the church lawn, the potluck dinner that is planned for Wednesday evening or a listing of those church members who are celebrating a birthday or anniversary during that particular week.

Now it's time for another hymn. Perhaps a special guest will sing a song or two to entertain us. Next, the offering plate is passed around and the collection taken. Finally, the real reason for our gathering together—the whole reason for the Sunday services—we finally make it to the sermon. Unfortunately however, because so much time has been spent on various traditions and formalities, the sermon may only last for twenty or thirty minutes. This is quite a far cry from the so-called pagan traditions which may last for days on end!

I have always felt that while society in general, and the Church in particular, might not agree with what witches or cultists believe, it is possible to learn from them. The growing popularity of the occult arts may be considered a definite sign of dissatisfaction with the traditional Church.

Marron points out that many young people are disillusioned by the mess the world is in and the apparent inability of society to do anything about it. This feeling of disillusionment, of powerlessness, often leads kids into the occult or Satanism in an attempt to tap into some kind of power.[8]

Later in the book, Marron provides additional insight into the problem of the Church failing to satisfy the needs of those who are searching for something more in their religion. His words should cause us to take notice. Marron later mentions people he has interviewed who, although raised in a religious setting, discover later in life that they wanted more from their religious system than turtle-paced songs or repetitive sermons.[9]

"Now hold on there," you may cry, "Our church services aren't like that! We sing lively songs, we even clap along sometimes! Our pastor is dynamic and energetic, and he doesn't limit his preaching to half an hour if the Lord has given him something to say."

Certainly many churches do not fit directly into the description above. A number of congregations, most notably the Pentecostal or Charismatic groups, do indeed tend to hold livelier Sunday services. But even these frequently get stuck in a set routine or begin to observe, without even realizing, an unwritten list of rules that dictate what kind of clothing should be worn, what kind of hairstyle is permissible, or how much make-up is too much.

Please understand, I am in no way suggesting that we allow the church to become a free-for-all experience where anyone can do anything he or she desires. Naturally, there is a time and a place for everything. For example, a Sunday morning church service is neither the time nor the place for a young woman to wear a tiny, skin-tight, black leather miniskirt with fishnet stockings, an overly-small T-shirt stretched to its limit, or two and a half pounds of jewelry topped off with a quarter pound of make-up.

But on the other hand, if such a person should enter your church next Sunday morning and sit down right beside you, loudly chewing her gum and filing her nails, shouldn't she be allowed to stay? Shouldn't she hear the

Word of God too? Isn't she a precious soul for whom the Lord Jesus Christ died? Or what about two or three teenage boys dressed in black leather jackets, torn blue jeans, and heavy metal rock-and-roll T-shirts. They may have long hair, an earring or two and maybe even a tattoo. But aren't they souls that Jesus truly loves and cares about? Aren't they precious in His sight? Don't they need to learn of Him?

Ask yourself right now, whether you are a pastor, a deacon, or a member of the congregation, would your behavior towards such people leave them with the impression that they are welcome to come back anytime, or would they leave knowing they had offended and disgusted you?

Several years ago I was told about a young boy who desperately wanted to attend a local church and learn more about the Lord. His parents however, strictly forbade him to go to the church. One evening, as was his custom, the youngster put on his running shoes, shorts and T-shirt and went jogging. He jogged right to the church! And they wouldn't allow him into the service. Apparently his attire was not suitable. Lord forgive us.

But it's only proper to get cleaned up and dress properly for church services. After all, it's God's house right? And it would certainly bother Him if we came to church in anything less than a three piece suit and tie or a conservative but attractive dress with heels, wouldn't it? I mean, surely the Lord couldn't love or appreciate anyone who would be so bold as to enter God's house in torn jeans and a leather jacket . . .

. . . God sees not as man sees, for man looks at the outward appearance, but the Lord looks at the heart (1 Sam. 16:7).

To show partiality is not good . . . (Prov. 28:21)

You (Jesus) are truthful and teach the way of God in truth, *and defer to no one; for You are not partial to any* (Matt. 22:16).

Do not judge lest you be judged (Matt. 7:1).

Of a truth I perceive that God is no respecter of persons (Acts 10:34 KJV).

For there is no respect of persons with God (Rom. 2:11 KJV).

> My brethren, do not hold your faith in our glorious Lord Jesus Christ with an attitude of personal favoritism. For if a man comes into your assembly with a gold ring and dressed in fine clothes, and there also comes in a poor man in dirty clothes, and you pay special attention to the one who is wearing the fine clothes, and say, "You sit here in a good place," and you say to the poor man, "You stand over there, or sit down by my footstool," have you not made distinctions among yourselves, and become judges with evil motives? . . . . If you show partiality, *you are committing sin* (James 2:1-4, 9; italics mine).

In my own ministry I make it a practice to wear clothing that is appropriate for the particular type of audience I am addressing. If I am speaking at a formal dinner, I certainly wear a suit and tie. If on the other hand I am speaking to a youth group, all of whom are wearing jeans and T-shirts, it would be ludicrous for me to walk in wearing a three piece suit, fancy silk tie, and shiny black shoes. Such apparel would cause me to stand out like the proverbial sore thumb and would only serve to alienate the vast majority of my listeners. Any adults who feel that such a group would respect a speaker simply because he is wearing a suit are sadly mistaken.

In fact, a dear friend of mine who pastors a Baptist church in New Brunswick, Canada, recently told me about an opportunity he had to address a secular high school class on the topic of "Change in the Church." He gave his talk and ended by pointing out that by far the most noticeable "change in the Church" that he noticed is that fewer and fewer young people are attending. He then used the opportunity to ask this class full of young people why that is. Their immediate response was to point to his tie! Several of the kids then went on to explain that they feel uncomfortable in the presence of suits and ties. They can't understand why they just can't be themselves.

I have personally wrestled with this issue myself for years. It has always been so tempting to just wear what is expected of me (a suit) and "go with the flow." Why not just put on the dressy clothes and keep everybody happy? The problem is that for years now the only people we have been "keeping happy" are the older church members who wear dressy clothes day in and day out anyway! We are most assuredly *not* keeping the young people happy!

This whole issue really came to a head for me one day as I was reading the Gospel of Mark, and I came to the place where Jesus and His disciples were approaching the synagogue. I got to the place where the Lord turned to James and John and the rest of the group and said, "Before we enter we must needs go to our own dwellings and changeth out of these common clothes. Maketh sure that ye showereth first, then putteth on thy best coverings. And do not forget to weareth a proper tie aroundeth thy neck lest ye offendeth another in the pew besideth thee!" (the Gospel According to Tradition).

But then it hitteth me—uh, *hit* me . . . Jesus never changed out of what He was wearing into something else before entering the synagogue! Neither did James or John or Peter or Matthew or Stephen! In fact, the only people mentioned in Scripture who made a big deal of their clothing were the scribes and Pharisees, And the Lord reprimanded them for it (Matt. 23:5, 25-28).

The point is simply this: the vast majority of church members, certainly the vast majority of pastors and definitely the vast majority of evangelists and televangelists wear suits—*and this puts a brick wall between the Church and the young people of today*. And the sad part is, we haven't got a single Scripture passage to defend our actions in this regard.

Not long ago I was speaking on the dangers of the occult and Satanism and I noticed four or five young men near the front row who didn't appear to be overly interested in what I had to say. About half way through my presentation I told the audience that I had had enough of my tight, confining, starchy double-breasted suit and tie, and I proceeded to remove the jacket and loosen the tie. As I did so, I looked directly at the young man who seemed the least interested and I asked if I could borrow his jacket. He handed it to me and I finished my message in a black leather motorcycle jacket! And the kids loved it. Afterward, every young person in the place came up to greet me and shake my hand. The whole atmosphere of the place changed dramatically just because I was willing to break a tradition in the church.

Quite frankly, if reaching a young person for Christ is as easy as putting on a pair of jeans instead of a suit, I'd gladly burn every suit I own. After all, what is more important, our image (that's what the Pharisees worried about) or the salvation of our young people?

Whenever I discuss this issue with fellow Christians the question is always asked, "What about our youth groups or special youth meetings? Aren't they good enough to reach the kids?" In all actuality, I truly believe that in many instances the "youth groups" are doing more harm than good. Think about it for a moment. . . . Just who attends these youth meetings anyway? For the most part such groups are made up of young people who are already believers or who are there only because their parents don't offer them a choice in the matter.

But where are the "bad" kids? Where are the ones who are getting into trouble with the law? Where are the ones who are courting disaster with drugs? Where are the ones who are dabbling in Satanism? *Where are the ones we should be trying to reach?* (Mark 2:17) Unfortunately, they probably don't even know about the "youth meeting" that is going on at your church. How could they know about it? It was probably advertised only within your church or on a Christian radio station or possibly on the religion page of the local newspaper.

But these kids don't go to your church and they don't listen to Christian radio stations and if they do happen to pick up a newspaper from time to time, they sure don't look at the religion page. Even if they did hear about your special youth meeting they wouldn't show up. Why? Because chances are your youth meeting is specifically geared (whether you realize it or not) to your own Christian youth. There is nothing there to interest the average sixteen-year-old who might be dabbling in the occult.

Occasionally we hear about powerful ministries reaching out to the young people of Detroit, Chicago, or New York with somewhat unorthodox measures. But too often we who are safely tucked away in our comfortable little rural or small city churches simply smile and say, "Thank goodness we don't have to go to such extremes to reach our young people here."

The fact of the matter, however, is that we are seeing an ever-increasing need for the smaller rural churches to begin emulating the efforts of the big city missions. This is largely due to the fact that there is so little for the teens to do in small agrarian areas.

A letter I received recently from a young man who had grown up on a farm in the Finger Lakes region of New York State sums this up for us. " . . . Satan's long arm of deception and intrigue reaches far out of the suburbs and cities without the benefit of despondent parents, cable TV, arcades, movie theaters, and groups of youth looking for something to busy their idle hands." So what *can* we do to be more efficacious in our struggle to win our young people for Jesus? Sean Sellers, a former Satanist presently awaiting execution for the murders of his mother, step-father, and a convenience store clerk, gave me this response to this important question, "Teenagers need to know more than just Jesus loves them. They need to know how to live a Kingdom life. They need discipleship. They need to know how to deal with the problems of life, how to set goals, how to succeed, and they need help making the important decisions that will affect their lives forever."[10]

Thankfully, there are several things that a pastor, youth worker, or active church member can do to reach out to teens who might otherwise not want to have anything to do with church. The first project you may want to attempt is to arrange various seminars, videos, or films on a regular and frequent basis. Sounds simple enough doesn't it? But there are some important factors to keep in mind.

First of all, the topics of the seminars or films should be of interest to the average *non-Christian* young person. Of course, a tremendous example of such a topic would be Satanism and/or the occult. Let's be realistic—a tough kid who's messing around with drugs and Satanism isn't going to come to a slide presentation of the Pastor's trip to Israel. I know a Word of Faith pastor who absolutely refuses to even mention the words "occult" or "Satanism" in his church much less show films on the topic. This type of attitude is so unfortunate. The time for burying our heads in the sand is long past. We have to start hitting these kids where they live instead of prancing around playing "little goodie two shoes," the cutesy Christian with the golden halo!

Secondly, don't go to the trouble and expense to advertise your event in the normal Christian outlets. Why bother? Is it the Christians you want to attract, or the lost? Instead, take out an ad in the local newspaper (*not* on the religion page), put up handbills around the city, or advertise on your local secular radio station.

Thirdly, and this is a vital point, avoid the temptation to preach or inundate your audience with Christianity. I don't think I have ever attended a Christian film or seminar that didn't start out with a few hymns or testimonies and quite frankly, there just isn't any need for it. The next time you attend such an event and the hymns start, take a look around at the young people. You'll see looks of disgust, looks of regret (they're sorry they ever walked into the place!), and looks of betrayal. We get the kids into the place by advertising it as a public meeting or a special event but the first thing we do once we've got them inside is start a church service!

Please understand, I am in no way suggesting that we compromise or hide the Gospel. I am merely pointing out that there are serious flaws in the manners and methods we are using to present it. I like to look at it in the same way that Jesus said we had to feed a hungry man's belly before we could even begin to feed his soul. This is a similar situation. We desperately need to gain the trust of the teens FIRST. We need to do everything we can to make them comfortable around us FIRST. We need to relax and be ourselves and let them do the same FIRST. Only after we have succeeded in these areas should we even consider bringing out our Christianity. A slow and comfortable approach is far better than a finger-shaking, look-down-the-nose, Bible-thumping attack.

It is also a good idea to hold such events in a secular location whenever possible (e.g., Y.M.C.A., public library meeting rooms, high school gymnasiums, etc.). This detail alone will help to put the average un-churched visitor at ease. Also, under no circumstances should a collection or offering be taken up at any such public functions. Finances should not even be mentioned. If we as Bible believing Christians can't raise the necessary funds to hold such meetings without putting our hands out to the lost, it may be time to re-evaluate our own commitment and dedication to the goal of helping kids in the first place. Nothing will turn off an already ill at ease visitor faster than a typical Christian appeal for money.

Another important undertaking is to ensure that your church library is well-stocked with solid Christian books on the cults, the occult, and Satanism. Young people become involved in the occult after reading books on the topic. Some have even immersed themselves in the black arts after their school teachers asked them to prepare reports on Satanism. We have to admit it, the occult is a fascinating subject for innumerable people, even Christians. Therefore we can do no less than to provide the curious seeker with a good selection of Bible based books and tapes on the various occult subjects. If we don't, the secular world is prepared to offer thousands of books that present Satanism and the occult in a positive, enticing way.

An idea, which is also commonly overlooked by the clergy, is to simply hold "parties" for the purpose of getting to know the kids in the area and allowing them to learn for themselves that we (believers) aren't as bad as they might have thought. You can advertise at the local high schools that all of the students are welcome to drop by the church on Friday night for free pizza, potato chips, and beverages. This isn't meant to be an evening of entertainment. There is no guest speaker, no rock band, and no film. The whole idea is for the kids to stop by and sit and chat with one another the same way they would if they were at a friend's house or on the school property during lunch break. The only difference is that the pastor, youth pastor, elders and deacons are there (*in jeans and sweat shirts!*) mingling and getting to know the kids.

In such a milieu it is crucial that you simply stop at a table for three or four minutes and chat with a particular group. *Do not preach* and *do not* make the common mistake of encouraging or even simply inviting them to come out to church on Sunday. That's all these kids ever hear from pastors and the minute they hear it from you they'll figure that the whole evening is an elaborate ruse to add members to the congregation. If the kids are interested, they know you have Sunday services. The whole point of an evening like this is to show the kids that we are human too. We have likes and dislikes. The pastor might be a big fan of professional football or baseball. The youth pastor might enjoy working on cars. Use this opportunity to remove the stereotypical masks that have been placed upon the Christian world rather than reinforcing the misconceptions the secular world has of us.

If you are really ambitious and truly interested in making a difference with the young people in your area, you might want to try something as radical as holding church services that are specifically designed for the younger adults and teens. You might want to use the Sunday evening service for this purpose or begin holding a service on Saturday morning or Thursday evening. Imagine the curiosity such a move would arouse in the community—a weekly church service where the preacher wears blue jeans and the congregation wears whatever they choose (within limits of course). The songs are lively and the sermon topics are especially interesting and useful for young people. You might have sermons based on what the Bible has to say about love, sex, murder, false cults, witchcraft, Satan, demons, and so on.

The normal Sunday morning service would continue without change for those who are accustomed to and comfortable with it. This new service however, would be geared mainly to the teen-agers. Adults should also be welcome to the services. In fact, it would probably be a good idea to have some adults at the services since it is not our goal or intention to segregate the kids. It may take a while before such an undertaking actually begins to show any signs of success. After all, you are toying with an age-old tradition (Sunday church services) but in the long run, if nothing else, the kids will see that you are willing to make some changes to accommodate them.

Now is an opportune time to point out the fact that "Young People's Church" or "Jr. Church" is not a workable solution to the problem of teens feeling uncomfortable in our churches. It is no secret that the teen-age years are awkward and confusing. The individual is no longer a child, but not yet an adult. This is an important fact to keep in mind when considering the aforementioned suggestions. The teen-ager is eager to grow up and is completely unwilling to take part in anything that even sounds like it is designed for youngsters (like Jr. Church). On the other hand, he is still too young to be overly interested in sermons designed with an adult audience in mind (e.g., finances, raising a family, etc.). So far the Christian Church has failed miserably in providing any sort of consistently attractive option for this sensitive age group.

Lastly, don't avoid preaching and teaching on the occult and Satanism during your Sunday services or Wednesday Bible studies. Too many pastors and preachers prefer to ignore the topics and, as mentioned earlier, this type of approach leaves the curious information seeker no alternative other than to obtain his facts from biased secular sources. Whatever you do, whether arranging seminars, preaching sermons on the occult or Satanism, buying books on the topics for the church library, etc., you absolutely must utilize extremely up-to-date information. This is particularly true when referencing rock-and-roll music. Do not make the all-too-common mistake of mentioning groups who were popular even a few short years ago. Rock idols come and go rather quickly and nothing loses the attention and respect of a teen-age audience faster than the realization that the speaker is misinformed or out of date regarding his information.

## A FEW WORDS ABOUT HALLOWEEN

There are several different and opposing opinions available regarding the question of Halloween. Should Christians celebrate it? Should we offer an alternative instead? Should we simply ignore it by not participating at all? Many Christian churches hold parties at the church on Halloween night in an attempt to offer a suitable replacement to the kids who aren't going door to door in search of candies. Some churches encourage the kids to attend the parties dressed as their favorite Bible character.

There are even churches out there who hold

get-togethers that closely resemble secular Halloween traditions! Costumes of any sort are permitted regardless of whether or not they reflect Christian values and beliefs, spooky music is played, and ghost stories are told. However, after several years of on-going research of the occult and Satanism, I make no apologies for my position that *Christians have absolutely no business or right to participate in the observance of Halloween in any way.*

When one seriously considers the fact that Halloween is held by many to be the most important satanic holiday of the year, I truly cannot understand how a sincere, Christ-loving, Bible-believing Christian can possibly justify *any* involvement in such a blatantly anti-Christian event.

I appreciate Johanna Michaelsen's comments on this matter. "So . . . should your family participate in the traditional Halloween celebrations? Absolutely . . . if you and/or your children are Witches, Satanists, Humanists, atheists, or anything other than born-again Christians (or Orthodox Jews). For a true Christian to participate in the ancient trappings of Halloween is as incongruous as for a committed cult Satanist coming from a blood sacrifice on Christmas Eve to set up a creche in his living room and sing 'Silent Night, Holy Night' with heartfelt, sincere devotion to Baby Jesus.

"Ephesians 5:1 admonishes us to 'be imitators of God.' Can you picture the Lord Jesus dressing up as Satan, or as one of the demons He cast out that week, or perhaps as a Druid priest, just because it was the Feast of Samhain and His disciples were giving a nifty party that night in honor of the tradition? . . . "[11]

Rather than feeling that we must provide our children with an alternative to the Halloween celebrations, why not be honest with them and explain to them what the night really represents and why as believers we have no interest in partaking in it.

On the other hand, Halloween presents a golden

opportunity for us to share the Gospel with numerous youngsters when they come to the door in search of a treat. Many excellent Gospel tracts are available, some of which are specifically written to be handed out on Halloween, which you can slip into the "trick-or-treat" bag of each youngster that comes calling. Halloween provides us with the only night of the year when dozens of strangers actually come to us rather than us having to seek them out and it would be senseless to pass up such a wonderful opportunity to spread the Good News about Jesus Christ!

## SOME EYE-OPENING OPINIONS

James "Jim" Hardy, a young man presently serving a life sentence with no chance of parole in the Missouri State Penitentiary for beating a friend to death as a sacrifice to Satan, didn't hold back when I asked him what he thought the main reason is for kids choosing to get involved in Satanism rather than the Christian Church.

"The Church has been turned into a joke! Hypocrisy is its biggest fault. Just a glance on the Church as a whole is enough to turn almost anyone away from Christianity. Does one really even need to ask 'why' teenagers are turning to Satanism rather than the Church?

"No one (especially a teenager) wants to worship a 'wimp'—but the Church constantly portrays Christ as a meek and humble pansy who got beat up all the time. Teens need to be taught the 'tough love' of God and Christ—Jesus was no 'wimp'! . . . Jesus drove the moneychangers out of the temple with a whip! He didn't just smack the floor a couple times and ask them to leave nicely. He *drove* them out—flipped over tables and *drove* them out!!!!

"Christ was a *radical* for God's true law in His time in the flesh. He is a radical for God's true law in our flesh today! We should not make God's laws void by the traditions of man.

"Through my dealings with young men in prison I have found that placidity will destroy our chances of bringing the masses to the foot of the cross."[12]

Sean Sellers offers some sobering thoughts, "If we're going to change it (the problem of Satanism among young people) we're going to have to start being a lot more responsible. We're going to have to get in touch with the youth, get in touch with the things that influence them, and we're going to have to start discipling those we do lead to the Lord.

"I don't think we'll ever make a difference, because I think most of the people in the Church are unwilling to give of themselves to the degree it will take to change things. Discipleship is a lot of work, a lot of giving. My experience has taught me that most people are too busy to accept such a responsibility. That's okay however, all we have to do is keep going the way we are and in two generations there won't be anymore problem. . . . There won't be anymore kids."[13]

# 7

# WHAT ABOUT CHRISTIAN ROCK?

Before attempting to respond to this urgent and inevitable question, I must point out that this is a very complex issue. There simply are no easy answers or self-evident facts. After responding to this very question at seminars, in articles and in correspondence, I have reached the inescapable conclusion that it is absolutely impossible to please everyone.

If we say that a song has to be along the lines of "Amazing Grace" or "The Old Rugged Cross" the older people in the church will cross their arms, lean back smugly in their chairs and say, "I thought so." But the kids won't be very happy. On the other hand, if we say that Christian rock bands like Petra or Stryper provide us with the ideal music for worshipping the Lord, the kids will applaud while the mature adults stamp out of the church never to be seen again.

Lastly, if we say that a happy medium can be found with the music of Keith Green, Don Francisco, or David Meece, the believers between the ages of twenty-five and thirty-five will be pleased but the kids won't accept it because it isn't loud enough and the older folks will refuse it because it isn't slow enough!

So what's the solution? What's the key? Just as with the issue of which church to attend, the question of which music is best boils down to a matter of personal preference and individuality. As much as the older folks argue against contemporary Christian music or Christian rock music, the bottom line is that fifteen-year-olds cannot be expected to leave Satanism and heavy metal rock music and immediately replace it with "Onward Christian Soldiers" or "How Great Thou Art."

Though none would ever dare to admit it, I truly believe that the main problem in this area is not so much a question of whether the Lord approves of the music as it is a question of whether or not *we* approve of it. It is unfortunate that some truly edifying and Christ-honoring music is being callously thrown into the waste basket by well-intentioned but woefully ignorant saints simply because it doesn't happen to appeal to them on a personal level. It is perhaps more unfortunate that countless numbers of such spiritual watchdogs have not so much as taken the time to listen to any of the artists they so vehemently criticize and condemn.

Bearing this in mind I respectfully encourage pastors, deacons, parents, and others to carefully consider contemporary Christian music in much the same way that you should examine the music of the secular world. Frankly, it is totally unacceptable for us to be uneducated or ignorant in either area. If rock-and-roll and heavy metal music is evil or dangerous, we should know why. And by the same token, if we believe that more up-beat or contemporary Christian music is wrong or unsafe, we should have valid reasons to support our opinions instead of simply dismissing it because we don't personally care for it.

One should never make dogmatic pronouncements on any topic if said topic has not been thoroughly researched and studied. However, most of the believers I run into who are adamantly opposed to any and all forms of contemporary Christian music have never even heard a sampling of the music they so boldly denounce. While I am not personally appreciative of some of the heavier Christian rock music available today, I do not hesitate to confess that I love contemporary Christian music. To be honest, I don't know what I would do if I had no alternatives to the slow, almost-operatic hymns that my grandparents used to enjoy.

Let me hasten to add that I do believe that some of the Christian rock musicians are going a little overboard in their efforts to provide an option to much of the trash that is passed off as music in the secular market today. In some cases it is difficult indeed to tell which bands are Christian and which are not.

It is my opinion that no professing Christian should appear on stage in skin-tight leotards that leave absolutely nothing to the imagination as to the physical development of the individual and no shirt. Obviously this is done in the secular world to promote sexuality and lust. I have no idea why it is done in the Christian world.

I have found that the following questions, if answered honestly and with an open mind, might help to let us know if what we are listening to is acceptable . . . or not.

1. Do the song lyrics glorify the Lord?
2. Do the lyrics agree with or contradict Scripture?
3. Do you feel closer to Jesus when you listen to the music?
4. Does the lifestyle of the artist reflect a true relationship with the Lord?
5. Would you listen to the same music if Jesus was sitting with you?

Once again we are faced with an issue that demands understanding on the part of adults. We simply cannot continue to tell our kids how wrong they are, how wrong their music is, how wrong their activities are, if we are not prepared to offer viable replacements.

" . . . They're sick unto death of the hypocrisy they see in so many of our churches. How can we expect them to be drawn to Christianity when 'Do as I say, not as I do' is presented to them as the unspoken motto of their parents and church leaders. These kids are not stupid. They rapidly figure out that if Christianity isn't working in the church it's not going to do much for them either. And they're rebelling against the mindless legalism and empty ritual that characterize so much of the church."[1]

All too often Christian churches tend to construct their own comfortable worlds within their four walls and subsequently lock out any and all differences or deviations from their distinctive pattern. Unfortunately, this usually causes the searching person on the outside to feel far too "different" or unacceptable to even dare to step inside.

Of course, this practice is diametrically opposed to the teachings of Jesus. Even the theological novice is well aware of what Jesus had in mind when He said that it was the sick and not the healthy that need the doctor (Matt. 9:12). But we continue to feed and nurture our own individual flock, many of whom have been saved for several years. Meanwhile, the runaways, the prostitutes, the Satanists lie down each night wishing deep within their hearts that the Bible stories they listened to as children were true—stories about Christian love and compassion, stories about Christ's followers helping others, stories about hope. However, to many of these people, they remain only stories. They can't become real because the Church is not telling them.

At least they can't come true while the vast majority of us, yes, I include myself, continue criticizing, judging, and condemning the lost. Not while we shake our heads at the hookers and the addicts on the streets and "thank God we're not like *them*." Not while we're busy playing church while countless souls enter a Christ-less eternity because we were too busy planning the next church picnic or potluck dinner. And the same thing applies to the music.

The church down the street might be totally against any and all music that incorporates drums or tambourines. The church at the other end of the city might feel that Christian rock is acceptable as long as the words are easily understood. The church right next door might teach that any music with a beat is a direct production of hell itself and that anyone who listens to it is destined for eternal torment.

But how many of the people who tenaciously cling to their opinions on Christian rock or contemporary Christian music have taken the time to seriously, sincerely, and open-mindedly study the issue and asked the Lord to lead them to a correct conclusion? So many issues in the Church today are handled with unbridled bias and the question of Christian rock is just another one on the list.

For example, those who believe in the gift of tongues today will generally read and study material only if it supports their already-reached conclusions. By the same token, those who do not accept the validity of tongues for the Church today will rarely consider material that opposes their position. There are those who believe that once a person is truly saved he or she can never again be lost. And there are those who believe that eternal salvation is conditional upon our continual observance of Christ's teachings.

The Church is divided over whether or not women should wear hats in church, whether or not they should wear slacks, and whether or not a woman should pastor a church. Sincere believers disagree on whether the Church should meet on Saturdays or Sundays, whether or not a Christian should drink alcohol, and whether or not a divorced believer should be permitted to remarry. And the list goes on and on.

But there is one thing that all of the aforementioned differences of opinion have in common—each of them concerns the believer, the Christian, the person who has already taken that infinitely important step of accepting Jesus Christ as personal Lord and Saviour. *Whether they disagree on peripheral matters or not, their eternal destiny has already been taken care of* (John 6:36; 3:16; 3:36; 1 John 1:9; etc.).

But the debate among Christians regarding Christian rock and/or contemporary Christian music is different in that it directly affects the non-Christian and has the undeniable potential of influencing an unsaved youth in his or her decision to accept, or reject, the Lord. Should we then compromise our beliefs, our doctrines, in order to reach the kids? Would the end results truly justify the means? The answer to both queries is a resounding "NO." However, we should most assuredly be willing to go to any lengths necessary to make absolutely sure that our teachings, our opinions and our beliefs are completely and totally supported by Scripture when we are dealing with an issue that has the ability to turn countless thousands of young people away from the Lord!

The sincere Christian who truly wants to see young people brought to a saving knowledge of the Lord should answer the following questions as honestly as possible:

1. Do I dislike Christian rock music simply because of my age?

2. Are my feelings regarding Christian rock based on prejudice or personal bias?

3. Is there anything inherently wrong with Christian rock music?

4. Are there any Scripture passages that clearly condemn or forbid Christian rock?

5. Would I be so willing to listen to hymns and classical Christian music if I was a teen-ager in the nineties?

6. Do I have any feasible alternatives to offer the kids?

Let's take a moment to consider what the Word of God has to offer on the subject.

First of all, and much to the surprise of many anti-rock activists, the Bible specifically declares that there is absolutely nothing wrong with loud music!

"Sing unto him a new song; play skilfully *with a loud noise*" (Ps. 33:3 KJV italics mine).

We also find that our music is to be solemn. However, it is necessary to realize that this does not mean sad or slow. It simply means that the music is to be serious and sincere.

"It is a good thing to give thanks unto the LORD, and to sing praises unto thy name, O most High: To shew forth thy lovingkindness in the morning, and thy faithfulness every night, Upon an instrument of ten strings, and upon the psaltery; upon the harp with a solemn sound" (Ps. 92:1-3 KJV italics mine).

Furthermore, the Word of God clearly indicates that there is nothing intrinsically wrong with rightfully using something that has been previously offered to idols. The Apostle Paul made this clear when he said that there was no longer anything wrong in eating meat that had been offered to idols. Obviously, it is our motives that count. It is not at all far-fetched to apply this same principle to rock music. Just because it is commonly regarded as "the Devil's music," there is no reason to feel that it cannot be turned around and offered to the Lord!

"I know and am convinced in the Lord Jesus that nothing is unclean in itself; but to him who thinks anything to be unclean, to him it is unclean"(Rom. 14:14).

Finally, and perhaps most importantly, God's Word clearly teaches that it is utterly unacceptable for us to judge another's taste in music.

"But you, why do you judge your brother? Or you again, why do you regard your brother with contempt? For we shall all stand before the judgment seat of God. . . . Therefore *let us not judge one another anymore,* but rather determine this—not to put an obstacle or a stumbling block in a brother's way" (Rom. 14:10, 13 italics mine).

Several years ago an article was written by Keith Green, which reflects many of the points considered in this chapter. As a talented and popular musician himself, Keith was able to provide valuable insights into this ongoing controversy. When I re-read the article recently I knew his thoughts had to be included in this book. I greatly appreciate the permission to do so, which was granted by his estate.

## CAN GOD USE ROCK MUSIC?[2]

This is a hard article for me to write. Mainly because I'm afraid people will think that my opinions would have to be prejudiced by the fact that I am involved in (what has come to be known as) "contemporary Christian music." As you might guess, the title of this article is no new question to me. Since I myself have been somewhat "guilty" of using the medium of rock, I have heard just about every opinion about it—and have received no limit of warning, exhortation, and outright rebuke from many a well-meaning soul. Since I take my negative mail very seriously—always reading each negative and corrective letter as a possible word or warning from God—I have had to listen closely to each argument—praying and thinking the whole thing through with eternal values in mind.

Although I have always wanted to address this subject publicly, I have only just answered the questions privately, seeking to avoid controversy. But now I believe the time has come for me to openly tackle this question, mainly because the Lord has been teaching me so much lately about motives and how *they* are the bottom line in just about everything!

Please realize that these are just *my* opinions. I am certainly no authority on scriptural truth—or music (except maybe my own). These are just some of the answers I have come up with after many years of studying this question with fear and trembling before the Lord. But like everything else, you should seek the Lord on your own for answers to difficult questions. I only hope to give you some things to think about.

### THE PREVAILING OPINIONS

There seem to be two different and widely opposite schools of thought concerning whether or not God can use something as questionable as rock and roll as a tool for evangelism, or even (forgive me!) in worship.

One line of reasoning believes that rock and roll, whether secular or "so-called gospel," should not ever be listened to, or used as a medium by Christians. The reason given is simply that it is "of the devil." There are many statistics and "proofs" used by adherents to this position to prove that rock music itself is the direct cause of everything from drug abuse to teen-age pregnancy. And most people who hold this view are sincerely convinced that anyone who indulges in the use of rock music in any form cannot truly be used or blessed by God.

The other school of thought is the one that believes that God can redeem and use anything—and just because rock music is so prevalent in the world doesn't mean that God's people can't use the same medium to reach those still lost in that world. After all (the people who defend this position say), "Christians are supposed to be 'in the world, and not of it!'[1] and didn't Paul say that he 'became all things to all men that he might save some?'"[2]

## THE VIEW FROM HERE

Of course, I have always leaned toward the second school of thought, but I think that sometimes this group has taken things a little too far, doing a lot in the name of "freedom" that I believe is grievous to the Lord, because it tends to stumble a lot of little ones. We should not forget that Paul also said, "Do not turn your freedom into an opportunity for the flesh."[3]

It is because of these abuses of freedom that I have chosen to remain silent on this issue. I have not taken up my pen to defend the "Christian rockers" because frankly, I've been just as much offended by most of what I've heard and seen as any sweet ole Christian grandma who accidentally stumbles into a blaring-loud gospel concert.

It isn't the beat that offends me, nor the volume—it's the spirit. It's the "Look at me!" attitude I have seen in concert after concert, and the "Can't you see we're as good as the world?" syndrome I have heard on record after record. Jesus doesn't want us to be as good as the world, He wants us to be better! And that doesn't mean excelling them in sound, style, or talent—it means surpassing them in value—in our motives for being up there on stage, in our reasons for singing our songs, and especially in *who* we're singing for! If there's anything wrong or worldly at all about so-called "Christian rock," it's the self-exalting spirit and attitude that comes across so loud and clear in many of the records and concerts today.

(Please don't get me wrong. I do not want to appear self-righteous, or to be saying—"All those musicians and artists should have such exemplary attitudes and motives as I do!" Believe me, I have struggled over these same things myself for many years, and these are things that the Lord has taught me for my own life and public ministry.)

## BUT WHAT ABOUT ALL THOSE "JUNGLE-RHYTHM" STORIES?

You've probably heard one of those stories about the missionary family that was stationed near a tribe of cannibalistic, voodoo warriors? Well, as the story goes, the missionary had a couple of teen-agers who just loved to listen to "Christian rock." And one day, as they were playing one of their albums up real loud, a witch doctor came running out of the jungle and said, "Why are you trying to call up devils with that music? Don't you realize that those are the same rhythms we use to contact demons in our rituals?" I've heard this story many times, and in many different forms, but it always seems to prove that, "There you have it! Rock and roll is a product of hell—even if it is called 'gospel rock'!" Now, I've always joked to myself that this story must have been started by some craggy old missionary who had been out on the field for twenty years and when he arrived back in the states, he just about died when he heard the latest gospel music. (Either that, or the witch doctor who came out of the jungle was a recent graduate from a conservative seminary!)

But seriously, I highly doubt that this story is true—and even if it is, it doesn't mean that all "music with a beat" will make your family need an exorcist. What we need to look into now is this question: Is there such a thing as "evil music"? To that question, I would have to answer a definite, "Yes!" but my reasons for calling some music "evil" may surprise you.

## WHAT IS *EVIL* MUSIC?

*"I know and am convinced in the Lord Jesus, that nothing is unclean in itself; but to him who thinks anything is unclean, to him it is unclean."*[4]

I do not believe that any kind of music is "evil" in itself. I mean that there are no such things as rhythms or chord structures or melody lines that were born in hell. The idea that the devil has invented certain styles of music so that he could capture the innocent young souls of today's youth is not only without foundation, but is the same kind of ridiculous tale that was told to young people by the church as recently as a generation ago—that "masturbation could cause blindness." Why try to scare the poor little guys into doing what's right? Why not deal with the real problem—selfishness!

The suggestion that there is such a thing as intrinsically (good or evil in itself) "good music" or "evil music" seems preposterous to me. I have been involved with almost every aspect of music my whole life, and I have witnessed the various effects it has had on me and other people—and I have to say that I have never once seen a case where music was the *direct cause of sin or wickedness in a person's life.*

On the other hand, I have seen music be used as a tool for selfishness and egotism in people's lives (as well as my own). I have also seen it be used to create sensual moods by people with lust and manipulation on their minds. I have seen rock groups that were admittedly worshippers of Satan, and were open practicers of black witchcraft, who employed music as a tool to mesmerize their audiences. Yes,

I must admit that it would appear to the casual observer that anyone involved with rock music could at least be charged with "guilt by association."

But all the examples I mentioned above have to do with the motives of the heart, not the music itself! That is why I believe that music, in itself, is a neutral force. Let me give you a better example.

Take a knife for instance. With it, you can cut bread, carve a roast, loose someone who's been bound by ropes, or you can do harm and even kill somebody. In other words, you can be creative and productive, or you can be destructive and murderous. The knife itself, when put in an atmosphere of hoodlums, becomes a weapon. But put it in a kitchen, and it becomes a tool that's useful, even necessary, for the preparation of nourishment for your family.

As another example, let's look at "David's dancing." The Bible says that King David was "dancing before the Lord with all his might!"[5] But today, people dance in bars and discos, and then afterwards, many indulge in alcohol, drugs, and illicit sex. Does that mean that dancing produces a desire for drugs, sex, and alcohol? You and I both know that, yes, movement of the body can excite someone. But someone has to have wicked desires to start with to have any outer stimulation increase those desires. I have seen Christians "dancing in the Spirit." I have also seen Christians dancing in the flesh. It wasn't the dancing that was evil, or the music they danced to, but the attitude and motive of their heart.

## SHOULD MEXICANS LEARN ENGLISH?

Now, we don't make the people of Mexico learn English before we preach the Gospel to them, do we? The only reason that I have ever used contemporary music at all in my ministry is because I believe it is the "language" of the young people. After I have received piles of letters saying things like, "I never would have listened to what you had to say, unless I had first been attracted to the music!"—I am convinced that the only way to reach those who love music is in their own language!

Have you ever heard the stories of how John and Charles Wesley took many of the popular "drinking songs" of their day and put Christian lyrics to them? And it didn't matter how much success they had in reaching sinners using these tunes—most of the people in the church absolutely deplored their methods!

And then the Salvation Army came along, and had the nerve to put hymns to marching music—and then proceeded to play and sing these "lewd songs" (as the traditional church of their day called them) out in the streets on Sundays! They even followed in the Wesley brothers' footsteps, taking tunes from the drunk-filled taverns, and "converting" them into worshipful choruses, or ringing appeals for people to surrender their lives to Christ! And never have there been so many "common people" converted in England than through the unorthodox efforts of those early "Salvation Soldiers."

Oh how harmless those melodies would sound now to our grandparents' ears. But their grandparents thought that the devil himself was on the loose with music-demons!

There are those today who still believe that we should use only nice, "wholesome" music to reach young people. Otherwise, (they say) we are only appealing to their sinful rebellion, and we will later find that any conversions resulting from the use of rock music were not really authentic after all. One well-known evangelist recently went so far as to say that, "No one has *ever* gotten a blessing from contemporary Christian music!"

This kind of reasoning is as narrow as that of the early missionaries to China. They thought that the best way to "Christianize" the people would be to teach them their European standards of dress and living, and thus "civilize" the heathen—as well as convert them. But a young and zealous missionary by the name of Hudson Taylor changed all that—he knew that the only way to reach people was with the truth of the Gospel. And he knew that it was wrong to add any cultural or "outward" conformity to the precepts of truth he so earnestly believed. And so he discarded his European clothing, and began to identify with the people he was trying to reach by dressing like them and adopting their customs. Although he was initially ridiculed and shunned by his fellow missionaries, his ultimate success proved that God was indeed leading him.[6]

## PLACING PEOPLE UNDER THE "LAW"

It seems that Paul had these same "cultural" problems in the early Church with those Jewish believers who wanted new converts to first embrace the Jewish law and customs before they could be considered Christians.[7] I believe that trying to change people's musical tastes, before we allow them to hear the truth, is just as wrong as it was for the Jews to try to push circumcision on the Gentiles as a necessary prerequisite for eternal life. The Bible is clear that we should put no stumbling blocks in the way of the people receiving God's precious gift of salvation!

## CONCLUSION: IT'S ALL IN THE MOTIVES!

I am convinced that the potential of reaching people for Jesus through the media—whether it be records, radio, movies, or television—is monumental, simply because these are the things that have, and continue to hold, people's attention. I truly believe that Christians who are completely sold out to God, using these tools, can bring people to their knees in repentance and lead them into the waiting arms of the Savior. But if their lives are not sold out—if their motives are mixed, and their hearts divided—then I only see ridicule and shame brought to the Gospel. And since this is the case so much of the time, it makes it hard and shines a bad light—even on those whose hearts are clean, and whose motives are pure.

I also want to say in closing that, yes, I do believe that the Holy Spirit is grieved by a lot of what is being passed today as "music ministry" and "gospel music"—not so much by the beat or content, but by the lack of commitment and anointing. But just because people with darkened hearts still use rock music as a medium for rebellion and self-exaltation, doesn't mean that the same style of music can't be used by people submitted to God to capture the attention of sinners, and lead them away from self—and to the throne of Christ!

After all, don't many cults use the same Bible that we cherish as God's Holy Word, and yet distort and twist the meaning "to their own destruction"?[8] And didn't the devil himself quote Scripture to Jesus? As you can see, a wicked heart can pervert even the most holy and beautiful of things. And in the same way, God can take even the filthiest of vessels and use it for His glory.[9] (Just look at you and me!) Believe me, if your heart is right, then your music will be right too. But if your heart is full of selfishness and pride, then even if you sing the sweetest hymn, your song will work death and not life. For . . .

*"A good man, out of the good treasure of his heart, brings forth what is good; and an evil man, out of the evil treasure, brings forth what is evil; for his mouth speaks from that which fills his heart."*[10]

1. John 17:11, 15-16.
2. 1 Corinthians 9:22.
3. Galations 5:13.
4. Romans 14:14.
5. 2 Samuel 6:14
6. *Hudson Taylor's Spirtual Secret*, by Dr. and Mrs. Howard Taylor; Moody Press, Chicago, IL 60610.
7. Galations 5:1-12.
8. 2 Peter 3:16.
9. 1 Corinthians 15:9-10
10. Luke 6:45.

# 8

# WHAT KIND OF MUSIC DOES THE DEVIL LISTEN TO?

*"Many rock stars who have succumbed to cults are pulling undiscerning young fans with them into their false beliefs. Sometimes well-meaning, other times as diabolical as Satan himself, these rock stars can greatly influence the lives of impressionable teens."*[1]

It seems that anytime we hear about kids getting messed up in Satanism rock-and-roll music is never too far away from the trouble. Numerous individuals who have ended their involvement with the occult or Satanism, myself included, are quick to point out that rock music (especially heavy metal) provided their initial introduction to the black arts. Close to 100 percent of the letters I receive from troubled kids who are writing for help or advice indicate that they are helplessly addicted to the music.

Why is this? I believe it is due to the fact that rock music goes well with drugs. Rock music goes well with sex. And rock music definitely goes well with Satanism.

Dr. Nelson Price expresses it this way, "It's hard to tell if the music industry exploits satanism or satanism exploits the music industry. Either way, through music, the themes of satanism—self-mutilation, assault, mayhem, suicide, drugs, murder, sex, and rebellion—have gone public. Freedom, irresponsibility, and violence recur in the message of this music."[2]

According to an article in *U.S. News and World Report*, it is estimated that teen-agers listen to 10,500 hours of rock music between grades seven and twelve alone. *This amazingly high figure is just five hundred hours less than the total time they spend in school over a period of twelve years!*[3]

If the information above doesn't sufficiently indicate just how prevalent rock-and-roll music is in the life of the average teen-ager, consider the following from *The Emerging Generation* by Reginald Bibby and Donald Posterski: "It is estimated that teenagers spend an average of six hours a day listening to music on their radios and stereos. Some of the time or perhaps additional time is spent watching rock videos, which have been experiencing explosive growth. *Researchers tell us that the very popularity of teenagers frequently depends on their familiarity with, and use of, popular music* "(italics mine).[4] Furthermore, Bibby and Posterski found that listening to music was *the number one leisure activity* of those polled while participation in a youth group ranked sixteenth. *Church or synagogue was seventeenth!*

Before proceeding, it must be pointed out that while much could be said about the blatant sexual lyrics of many rock musicians or the overt consumption and promotion of narcotics and/or alcohol as well as many other questionable aspects of rock culture, for the purposes of this treatise we restrict ourselves to the area of occult/Satanism as it is promulgated and promoted through rock-and-roll. Certainly this is not meant to imply that Satanism is the only negative by-product of the rock music industry. Quite the contrary. However, since this is not meant as an exhaustive analysis of rock-and-roll or heavy metal, we would do well to limit our study of it to that which is directly related to the subject matter of this book.

After giving my life to the Lord and beginning to

look at things from His point of view, I couldn't believe just how conspicuous many of the rock performers were with regard to their involvement with Satanism, witchcraft, or other occult practices. We certainly have come a long way from the horrible witch trials in which some were mercilessly tortured and killed. But I can't help but wonder if perhaps we have come just a little too far.

The particular bands that I listened to as a Satanist flagrantly sang about the devil and various black arts. When I got saved I shook my head and thought to myself, "It can't get any worse than that!" But it has. In fact, satanic messages and innuendos have become so prominent in the world of rock-and-roll that a new category of music has recently been created. This new division is known as *"Black Metal Music"* and it specifically refers to the numerous heavy metal bands that are known for their affinity with evilness, death, and Satanism.

It is common practice for those who oppose such bands to list several of the more prominent offenders for the benefit of parents who desire examples of which bands they need to be aware of. However, we purposely avoid doing so here for two important reasons. First of all, since it is next to impossible to keep up with the constantly changing roster of big name rock bands who might be the hottest item one day but virtually unknown the next, we feel that it is better not to mention any groups by name lest we give the false impression that any bands not included in such a listing are consequently acceptable.

Secondly, and perhaps most importantly, as we mentioned in chapter 5, it is vital that parents begin to take an active interest in the music their children are listening to and such an interest should involve far more than simply searching through a son's record collection to find out whether he is listening to the bands named on a particular list. The parent should be willing to take the time to carefully consider all of the albums, tapes, and compact discs their children purchase *regardless of whether or not they have been specifically warned against the particular artists.*

## IT'S JUST A GIMMICK TO SELL RECORDS

A number of the recording artists who use occult trappings claim that it is nothing more than hype. They may sing about Satan or use occult symbols on their album covers or stage sets but it is only done as a gimmick to sell records and gain popularity. While this could be true, the problem lies in the fact that hundreds of thousands of impressionable kids who look up to these performers are unaware of that fact and are falling for their dangerous charade hook, line, and sinker.

As we saw in chapter 2, some kids become involved with Satan worship not because they are personally interested in it, but because they wish to imitate their rock idols. Therefore, whether or not the musician is actually a Satanist himself, if that is the image he portrays to his fans, many will perceive him as being actively involved in that which he promotes through his music.

Surprisingly, there are also those people who claim that rock-and-roll music has nothing whatsoever to do with Satanism and vice versa. But the fact that countless Satanists openly admit to being die-hard fans of black metal music, along with the fact that numerous kids decide to try Satanism after being exposed to it through rock music, cannot be brushed aside or ignored.

## BUT WHAT'S SATANIC ABOUT THE MUSIC?

The ongoing struggle between moralists (and Christians) and rock music has been waging for decades. People thought that Elvis Presley's gyrating pelvis was so lewd and obscene that some actually thought he was the devil incarnate. Jerry Lee Lewis raised more than a few eyebrows with his wild on-stage persona. The sixties provided preachers with quite a lot to speak out against when the music began to take on certain aspects of rebellion and anti-war messages along with the prevalent drug use among many musicians and fans.

Rock music has always had a reputation for being

controversial. Because of this, many people mistakenly assume that we are merely witnessing another fundamentalist uproar against the evils of rock-and-roll. The old folks are making too much out of nothing and pinning the rap for teen-age occult involvement and suicide on the innocent shoulders of modern music.

Is this the case? Is rock music just a convenient scapegoat on which to load our complaints and insults or is it truly something for us to be concerned about? It is frightening to realize that Eric Barger's *Rock Music Rating System* includes *over 325* bands or artists who are known for their references to or involvement with various aspects of the occult, participation in or glorification of a non-Christian cult, satanic/demonic themes and abuse of or contempt for God, sacred things or Christianity. This information is based on "song lyrics, album cover artwork, videos and stage sets as well as from magazine articles and interviews that portray the lifestyles of those listed."[5]

While conducting research for this book, I had various teen-agers complete a brief questionnaire outlining some of their feelings toward rock-and-roll music. Some of their answers were shocking. When asked what would happen if they suddenly had to stop listening to rock music, and given the following choices—"It wouldn't matter," "I wouldn't like it but I'd get used to it," or "I would seriously consider suicide"—an incredible 14 percent chose the latter. One such respondent is only thirteen-years-old! When asked what they would be willing to do to meet their favorite rock performers the answers were incredible. A small sampling follows:

I would break my leg.

twelve-year-old female

Pay anything. Do anything. Give anything.

seventeen-year-old male

I would do just about anything in the world.

eleven-year-old female

Camp out for days in snow and rain.

fifteen-year-old female

Do back flips naked.

fifteen-year-old female

I would kill.

fifteen-year-old male

In response to the important question as to whether or not rock-and-roll music influences their beliefs or opinions about religion, 14 of those polled indicated that it does. When they were asked if they felt that rock performers who sing about Satan really believe what they are saying (as opposed to using Satanism/occult as a gimmick to sell records), 41 percent said yes. Interestingly, when asked how they felt about those bands that sing about Satan and the occult, more than half of them were completely against it. Individual responses went from "I hate it" and "I think it should be banned" to "They should all be shot."

The following information is offered as merely the proverbial "tip of the iceberg" to illustrate some of the offensive characteristics of today's rock-and-roll music. "The first words of greeting from vocalist Bruce Dickenson (Iron Maiden) to a 1986 concert crowd in Portland, Oregon, were 'Welcome to Satan's sanctuary!'"[6]

"During the audience participation section of a television show I did with the rock group Metal Church, a young man stood up and confirmed some shocking facts that we were pointing out through his experience at a BOC [Blue Oyster Cult] concert. It seems that they take time out from the music to promote and proselytize for their religion . . . satanism!"[7]

"Using the international sign for deletion (the red line diagonally through an object inside a circle), the Dead Kennedys say, 'Let's stamp out the church!'"[8]

"While in his original group, Black Sabbath, which was formed in 1969, Ozzy Osbourne joined in black masses before concerts. . . ."[9]

"Daryl Hall of Hall and Oates, voted 1984's Favorite Pop Group by the American Music Awards, is a dedicated follower of Aleister Crowley."[10] Crowley was a notoriously evil man who called himself "The Beast 666." He is now revered by many as a sort of grandfather of modern Satanism and black magic.

"When fans were asked just what they would do to meet Motley Crue, the answers ranged from 'sacrifice of wives and children' to one fan saying she would 'tear out her mother's heart with her bare hands and eat it raw!'"[11]

Rock superstar Madonna says that she likes the feeling of a crucifix around her neck because of the naked man on it (Jesus)![12]

"That rock group (AC/DC) also seems to have played an inadvertent role in the murder spree of Richard Ramirez, the so-called Night Stalker, who spread terror throughout Southern California in the summer of 1985 by sneaking into homes during the dead of night and mutilating and murdering the inhabitants. Ramirez, who spray-painted Satanic pentagrams on the walls of some of his victims, was a self-styled Satanist and an avid AC/DC fan, and it is said that he took their song 'Night Prowler' as the inspiration for his nocturnal blood orgies."[13]

"VANDALISM RELATED TO THE OCCULT. Burlington, Ont. (CP) Four youths have been charged in connection with the occult-related vandalism of St. Paul's Presbyterian Cemetery that caused more than $50,000 in damage, police said today.

"The youths told police they knocked over about 60 headstones Monday *after listening to heavy-metal rock music laced with lyrics about the devil and the occult*, said Sgt. Dave Pruitt of Halton Regional police.

"'It was learned that a fascination with the occult drew their attention to the cemetery,' said Pruitt. '*They listened to lyrics about cemeteries and grave robbing*'" (italics mine).

"RAMPAGING YOUTHS UNDER INFLUENCE

OF DRUGS, MUSIC. Sarnia, Ont. (CP) A teenager convicted today of wounding a donkey with a knife had consumed LSD and alcohol *and was influenced by rock musicians* the night he and another teen took part in a grisly animal slaughter.

"In a statement read to district court Judge Michael Meehan, Peter Mitchell, 18, of nearby Point Edward admitted he and another teenager were responsible for harming animals in a spree that left birds beheaded and a pony slashed to death at Canatera Park Children's Farm on March 1, 1985.

"A goat and pigeons were also wounded, assistant Crown attorney Mary Nethery said.

"Defence lawyer Joseph Donahue said his client '*was influenced by certain rock musicians and what they do with animals and birds on stage*' the night he took part in the slaughter.

"At one point, Mitchell said, he knocked a pigeon down and the other teen 'bit its neck off.'

"Later that night, he said, he 'just stood there' as his accomplice slashed a goat and a duck.

"When asked by police why he and the other youth injured the animals, he replied: 'I don't even know why it happened'" (italics mine).

## ROCK MUSIC IS GETTING WORSE!

As we have already noted, there has been some startling changes in the music world over the past three or four decades. Studies have been conducted, interviews and surveys have been carried out, and even psychiatrists, psychologists and social workers have found it necessary to research the rock-and-roll enigma and share their views with concerned parents and others.

The music and messages of popular bands of the 50s and 60s, which once caused parents to genuinely fear for their children, has paled in comparison to what goes on in rock music today.

To illustrate this procession from bad to worse we

need only compare the names of some earlier bands to bands which are popular today.

### Popular Performers of the 50s, 60s & 70s

| | | |
|---|---|---|
| The Coasters | The Drifters | The Crests |
| The Angels | Kingston Trio | Chubby Checker |
| The Drifters | The Chiffons | The Happenings |
| The Orioles | Fats Domino | The Kingsmen |
| Shangri-Las | Righteous Brothers | Gallery |
| Lovin' Spoonful | The Beach Boys | Jan & Dean |

Innocuous band names like those listed above have changed to reflect the present state of music and musical tastes. Today we find groups with names like . . .

### Popular Performers of the 80s & 90s

| | | |
|---|---|---|
| Megadeth | Iron Maiden | Black Sabbath |
| Motley Crue | Slayer | Violence |
| Slaughter | Poison | Skid Row |
| Beggars & Thieves | Faith No More | Lynch Mob |
| Annihilator | Coroner | Massacre |
| Manic Street Preachers | Mortician | Obituary |

If the actual group names don't illustrate my point clearly enough, perhaps a similar consideration of some popular song titles will help to clarify the matter . . .

### Popular Song Titles From the 50s, 60s & 70s

| | |
|---|---|
| "Blue Suede Shoes" | "I'm Walkin'" |
| "Peppermint Twist" | "Dock of the Bay" |
| "Put Your Head on my Shoulder" | "Yakety-Yak" |
| "Crimson & Clover" | "Nice to be With You" |
| "Sixteen Candles" | "Palisades Park" |
| "Surf City" | "Sh-Boom" |
| "Little Honda" | "California Girls" |

**Some Song Titles From the 80s & 90s**

"Talk Dirty to Me"
"Number of the Beast"
"Suicide Solution"
"Sacrificial Suicide"
"Thou Shalt Kill"
"Body Bag"
"Sacrificial Annihilation"
"Bring Your Daughter to the Slaughter"
"Highway to Hell"
"Dead Child's Eyes"
"Chopped in Half"
"Powers of Hate"
"Multiple Stab Wounds"
"Dying"

With nothing more than the above information in mind there can be no argument that rock-and-roll music has come a long, long way over the years. The problem, however, is that it's been heading in the wrong direction.

If what you have read thus far regarding the world of heavy metal and black metal music has shocked or angered you, you may want to take a few deep breaths before proceeding. Two of the newest forms of rock music are known as "Grindcore" and "Death Metal." Both are notorious for completely disregarding normally acceptable limits of good taste and acceptable behavior. The bands routinely sing (or is it scream?) about such things as death, massacres, suicides, and human sacrifice with song titles like "Reek of Putrification," "Weltering in Blood," and "Cannibalistic Dissection." One member of the band Deicide, Glen Benton, claims to have been a practicing Satanist since the tender age of ten when he was introduced to it by some of his cousins. When asked why he throws blood into the audience at his concerts, Benton said, "Fans love it. Have you ever smelt rotting guts? I love the stench of guts, it gives me a hard-on! And if those fans pick up the lifestyle, they'll just be improving themselves, making themselves strong and smashing the weak."[14] The name of the band seems to sum things up concisely. Deicide means "the killing of a god."

Steve DiGiorgio, bassist for the band Sadus, says,

"This music isn't really *made* by twisted people, it's the people who buy it who are f — ed in the head. They're the ones who go home and tear their houses apart. . . . I rarely listen to music like this."[15] Grindcore band Morbid Angel is led by Trey Azagthoth (Azagthoth is the name of the Sumerian god of war and disorder), who bit himself and drank his own blood at a New Music Seminar in New York. Azagthoth later explained, "When I do something like that onstage, it's not something I'm parading or some kind of gimmick. . . . It's just personal expression. If I feel like drinking blood, I'll do it."[16]

Another Grindcore band called Carcass is known for its extremely crude song titles, among them, "Excoriating Abdominal Emanation," "Cadaveric Incubator of Endoparasites," and "Swarming Mass of Infected Virulency."

Ironically, the Christian Church has become somewhat of a joke to those involved in the rock music industry for continuing to preach against such comparatively mild performers like Judas Priest, Aerosmith, and the Rolling Stones. Compared to Grindcore and Death Metal bands, such bands are teddy bears!

## CENSORSHIP AND RECORD LABELLING

Many people believe that rock-and-roll albums should carry a warning label on the cover if they contain offensive or obscene lyrics. With only a casual consideration, this may sound like the perfect solution to the problem of youngsters being exposed to pornographic or satanic content. However, it may do more harm than good.

An article in the *Cincinnati Enquirer* entitled, "Warning Labels Send Records up the Charts," explains that ". . . If there's a choice involved between a stickered and a sanitized version of the same album, kids almost always choose the 'street version' because it indicates provocative—read hip—content. . . ."[17] The article goes on to provide the following comparison of sales. The labelled version of the controversial album *As Nasty as They Wanna Be* by 2 Live Crew was the sixth best-selling album at the time the article was written while the "clean" version ranked at number forty-five. The "adult" version of the album *Walk Like a Panther* by LL Cool J outsold the clean edition by a margin of 10 to 1.

## EASY TO GET PAST LABELS

Although certain warning labels forbid the sale of the album to minors, it is a simple matter for kids to get them. Just as countless teens convince older siblings, friends, or even total strangers to purchase beer or cigarettes for them, they can easily have someone else purchase records or tapes for them.

The executive director of the Parents Music Resource Center, Jennifer Norwood, believes that warning labels are a good thing and that they do not help to increase record sales. However, advertisers have known for quite some time that even negative publicity is still publicity.

A tremendous example of this theory can be seen in the ruckus caused by the blasphemous movie, *The Last Temptation of Christ*. Thousands of Christians blocked theater entrances, waved banners, wrote letters to newspapers and television stations and so on. Unfortunately, most critics and reporters seemed to feel that the movie was nothing special and that it would have come and gone quickly if not for all the picketing and complaining. Numerous people said that they never would have bothered to see the movie if their curiosity hadn't been so stirred-up by all the controversy.

I remember a similar situation several years ago when a particular issue of a popular men's magazine was banned here in Canada. Due to the television, radio, and newspaper reports on the controversial magazine, sales skyrocketed before anyone had the chance to remove the offending issue from the newsstands!

I believe that the same thing is destined to happen with regard to warning stickers on rock albums. Some parents have complained that, if anything, the warning labels have only served to arouse the curiosity and mischievousness of their kids. Theoretically, the stickers are placed on album covers to warn parents about the content of the album. This would be fine if parents were the ones who actually went into the stores and purchased the albums. But in most cases they are not. Generally speaking, kids save their allowance money for albums or earn their own spending money with part-time jobs. Consequently, they buy their own albums without their parents ever setting foot in the record store. We've already considered the fact that most parents simply don't make an effort to know what their kids are listening to or buying. Warning labels may be just a vain attempt to make us feel better without us having to actually do anything.

**WHAT ABOUT FREEDOM OF SPEECH?**

The argument against record labelling, or any other kind of control, is based mainly on the various rights provided all citizens in the Constitution. The problem however, seems to be the question of where to draw the line. When our founding fathers penned the Constitution, did they believe it would be acceptable for popular performers to sing about murder, suicide, or graphic sexual acts?

Should it be legal for singers and songwriters to spew forth twisted lyrics that would be considered pornographic if they appeared in print, with no constraints whatsoever? Quite frankly, I had hoped to be able to quote some examples of popular song lyrics in this book so that my readers would be able to see for themselves just how bad the situation really is. But I couldn't. You see, although we hear how the music "isn't bad," and "the lyrics are merely artistic expressions," the simple fact is that in many cases the lyrics are so filthy that they simply cannot be quoted in newspaper articles or in books like this one.

This was mentioned in an article which covered the testimony of rock musician Frank Zappa before the Senate Judicial Proceedings Committee in Maryland. When referring to what occurred at the meeting the author says, ". . . Many of them recited a litany of explicit sexual lyrics—*much of it too graphic to repeat in a family newspaper*—as evidence of the kind of pornography that the government should keep children from hearing in music or seeing on album covers"[18] (italics mine).

I couldn't help but take special notice of a particular comment made by Mr. Zappa during the aforementioned proceedings: "No sound that comes out of your mouth will send you to hell."[19] This comment, of course, is quite a sharp contrast to the words of Scripture, "But what proceeds out of the mouth, this defiles the man" (Matt. 15:11 see also 12:36). As with everything else we have considered thus far, there are no simple answers or quick fixes. Anything that deals with the interpretation of the Constitution necessarily becomes a complicated issue.

Meanwhile, musicians, publicists, record companies, and politicians fight it out. You can do your part by taking the time to phone or write to radio stations if you hear them playing blatantly offensive songs. Take the time to talk to managers of record stores if you notice obscene lyrics or illustrations on record albums or posters, especially if such materials are within the reach of minors. But more than anything else, take the time to check into the kinds of things *your own kids* (or grandchildren) are buying into. Don't be oblivious to what is happening under your own roof.

## HEXAGRAMS, PENTAGRAMS AND MORE — ALL FOR THE LOW, LOW PRICE . . .

Another fairly recent development which caused my jaw to drop to the floor when I first noticed it was the open sale of occult jewelry and paraphernalia in certain rock magazines.

A popular rock music magazine recently featured a full-page advertisement for a mail order company in Florida. The ad offered various styles of bracelets, necklaces, earrings, pins and key chains.

Among the items available we found:

5 inverted (upside down) crosses

9 pentagrams (or variations thereof)

39 miniature human skulls
3 images of the Grim Reaper

Other items included an anarchy symbol, two Egyptian ankhs, a noose, nine swords/daggers, a battle-axe, marijuana leaves, a demon head and two vulgarities. Amazingly, of the ninety-five items shown in the ad, 65 percent are related to the occult or death. Another ad in the same publication (placed by a different company) features T-shirts, necklaces, rings, earrings, and removable tattoos. Among the items available we found:

2 inverted crosses
3 pentagrams
53 miniature human skulls/skeletons
3 images of the Grim Reaper
1 rotting corpse
2 anarchy symbols

Additional items pictured in the ad include an assortment of knives, swords, axes and other weapons, two Egyptian ankhs and marijuana leaves. Of the 128 items pictured, 56 percent are related to the occult or death. Still another ad features jewelry with colorful names such as:

Pentagram Pendant
Alchemist Pendant
Death Ring
Screaming Demon Pendant
Ring & Skull Buttons
Spirit of Death
Witch Doctor Earring
Grim Reaper Ring
Death Mask

Surely these advertisements for satanic and occult jewelry are another sign of the times we are living in.

Several years ago, when I myself was involved in Satanism, it was necessary to make our own inverted cross necklaces by purchasing a regular crucifix, drilling a hole in the bottom end of the cross, and running a chain through the new hole so that the crucifix hung upside down. It was next to impossible to simply order pentagrams, ankhs and inverted crosses through the mail just a few years ago but such items are incredibly easy to get today.

Even as this book goes to press, we are seeing more and more outrageous developments in rock music. So much so, that it is almost impossible to keep up with what is happening. Nevertheless, as responsible adults, as parents, and above-all, as Christians, we have the responsibility to do whatever we can to help others steer clear of the devices of the enemy. Why not purpose in your heart right now to no longer simply "hate" rock music, or criticize rock music and rock musicians, but to set aside prayer time each and every day for those who are trapped by it.

Don't forget to pray for rock musicians as well. So often we get wrapped up in our debates and crusades and our criticisms that we tend to forget about the souls of the people we're complaining about. Underneath the leather and the tattoos, under all that make-up and jewelry there is a precious human soul that the Lord Jesus died for. And Jesus loves them. That's an important point. No matter how upset we get about the music and its message. No matter how frustrated we get about what it's doing to our kids. No matter how disgusted we become with the satanic images and symbols and song lyrics . . . Jesus loves them. And so should we.

Eric Barger sums this up well. "As Christians, we are to know from experience, that prayer is life-changing and earth-shaking (see James 5:17 for just one example). With that knowledge we are to act, that is to pray, using the instructions God has given us through His Word. We will never understand the power of prayer until we begin praying regularly. Most of us know these things. However, I am alarmed about a poll I've been conducting at our seminars. I ask the crowd, 'How many of you are actively praying for a rock musician?' Most nights not one hand is raised, indicating to me that we have a real problem.

"Like them or not, the rock musicians are affecting thousands, even millions, of young people and young adults adversely for the devil's glory. And even more than that, those musicians are souls Jesus bled and died for on Calvary. Christ paid the price for them, they are being used as pawns for Satan, millions of people hang on their every move and *we are not even praying for them.*"[20]

# 9

# FANTASY ROLE PLAYING GAMES:

# AN INTRODUCTION TO THE OCCULT?

Contemporary writings on the topics of Satanism and the occult invariably mention at least two factors that appear to lead some individuals, particularly young people, into the occult: heavy metal rock music and fantasy role playing games (FRPs). Why is this? What can a game possibly have to do with Satanism or other questionable practices?

The answers to these queries are not simple. It may help the reader to understand the connection between "games" and occult involvement when he or she understands that Fantasy Role Playing games like Dungeons & Dragons are substantially different from traditional games such as chess, checkers, or Snakes and Ladders. Unlike these, FRPs are played mainly in the minds of the players rather than on a game board. Due to the fact that each game is basically limited only by the imagination and enthusiasm of the player, it is common to hear of games that continue for extended periods of time. While a simple game of checkers might take anywhere from ten minutes to an hour, a detailed game of Dungeons & Dragons may go on for several days or weeks or in some cases, years.

But what difference does any of this make? In our attempt to answer this question, let's begin at the beginning. Dungeons & Dragons was born in the mid 1970s when it was created by Gary Gygax and Dave Arneson. The game is manufactured in Wisconsin by TSR Hobbies Incorporated, a company that began in 1974. Interestingly, when the game was first introduced to the marketplace, its main audience was made up of adults. However, this changed when the game began to catch on at high schools and junior high schools. Today Dungeons & Dragons (D & D) is popular with kids who are too young for junior high.

The game itself consists of strange-looking dice and books or manuals. Important details of the game such as the strength, intelligence, wisdom, and so on, of each individual character are determined by several rolls of the dice. Dice rolls also determine other factors such as the "hit points" of each character, which represent the amount of damage he can sustain as well as what weapons and armor the character is supplied with.

The game is controlled by an individual who is generally more experienced with D & D than the others. This player is known as the Dungeon Master or DM. The main role of the Dungeon Master is to design and prepare the adventure and setting of the game for those who are actually going to play. The DM chooses such details as the terrain, odors, various creatures and beasts and so on. While all of this may sound as simple as sitting down with a pen and paper and jotting down a quick list of particulars, the process is extremely involved. It may take as many as forty-eight hours to plan and prepare a game properly—given the extreme attention to detail that is demanded by most D & D players and Dungeon Masters. It is reported that at least one individual has become so involved in the game that she found it necessary to leave her job in order to have time to "work" full-time as a Dungeon Master. The game requires a minimum of two players but is usually played by a small group (approximately five players).

After the Dungeon Master explains the particulars and setting of the game he has created, play begins.

Pat Pulling mentions in her book, *The Devil's Web*, that the play is described so vividly "that the participants actually can visualize it in their minds, almost as if they were watching it on a giant movie screen. Since it is imperative for the players to 'become one' with their characters, the players feel extremes of emotions relative to the action of the game. They experience anger, frustration, fear, elation, triumph, and despair."[1]

The game usually includes pretended criminal acts committed by the characters—torture, rape, and theft. The object of the game is to survive, and almost anything the character decides he needs to do in order to survive is fully accepted. I have mentioned that Fantasy Role Playing games are essentially played in the minds of the players and are therefore chiefly limited only by the creativity and imagination of the individual. For this reason the game is attractive not only to those who feel there is nothing better to do with their time than play games, but those who are highly intelligent and talented as well see the games as stimulating and challenging. It is also important to note that such games can become quite addictive as the player becomes more and more attached to his or her character. There are those who believe that such emotional attachments might lead to suicide when a player sees his character, which has become his alter-ego by this point, destroyed in the game.

Because of the complexity and necessary devotion of time to the preparation, planning, and playing of the game, some players tend to over-identify with their imaginary characters and become totally absorbed by the fantasy to the point of being unable to differentiate between it and reality. Because of their own involvement in the game, many players will not notice any changes in their personality. Friends and family, however, often notice a change.

## WELCOME TO THE OCCULT

Another major concern with FRPs is the abundant use of occult terminology and belief systems. Among the more questionable aspects of such games we find occult magic and spell casting, communication with spirits of the dead as well as the practice of summoning demons, soul travel or astral projection, and affiliation with occult powers or deities.

In addition to this, the names of (real) magic or occult orders can be found in at least one game while others actually include instructions on how to form one's own magic or occult order. Some Fantasy Role Playing games provide the player with accurate and precise instructions regarding sacrifices—even going so far as to provide actual calendar dates for same. Many games strongly encourage the player to thoroughly investigate pagan, Eastern, and occult cultures from which the mythologies and deities of the game are drawn. Not surprisingly, after having done so, some players become active in the non-Christian religions they have been introduced to through the game.

Dungeons & Dragons is considered by many to be an exceptionally effective introduction to the occult. One occultist considered the game to be such a tremendous way to introduce players to the occult that he wrote a book telling players how to progress from the game to actual occult involvement.[2]

## BLOOD, GUTS & DEATH

While many researchers and writers tend to concentrate mainly on the occult nature of FRPs, it is also well worth noting the extreme violence and lack of compassion that is a fundamental aspect of the games as well. In the FRP game, Arduin Grimoire, for example, a dice roll of thirty-seven to thirty-eight indicates a hit to the crotch or chest. The result is genitals and breasts being torn off. A dice roll of one hundred indicates a hit to the head and results in the victim's head being "pulped and splattered over a wide area."[3] Dungeons & Dragons refers to creatures that pillage, rape, loot, and kill.[4] We are also told that death comes in many ways but death due to combat is the most common.[5] The Advanced D & D Handbook informs us that life, freedom, truth, and the like are without value.[6] Some believe that such blatant violence and disregard for human life, coupled with occult and satanic belief systems could have disastrous results in numerous cases. Instructions for murder in the D & D Dungeon Master's Guide actually call for the player to develop a complete and detailed plan for carrying out assassination (p. 75), all in an imaginative mode of course.

It appears this casual approach to violence and murder has spilled over into the real lives of players on more than one occasion.

## DEATHS ARE REAL, NOT FANTASY

A seventeen-year-old is convicted of killing a policeman. According to a report on 23 October 1983 in the Los Angeles *Herald Examiner*, a friend of the family views the boy's preoccupation with science fiction, television, and especially the intricate, "seductive" D & D as a catalyst for disaster. She said, "It's like opium, destroying the barrier between life and fantasy."

Seventeen-year-old Larry Swartz is convicted for the murder of his parents. Swartz later claimed that the only problem with being in jail was that he would not be able to do what he loves most, namely, play Dungeons & Dragons.

The *Evangelist* reported a suicide victim in Madison, Ohio, was obsessed with D & D, according to his sister who related her story in the *Lake County News* (30 April 1983). She said that although she knew her brother had an unhealthy obsession with the game, she was not aware that he was practicing auto-erotic hanging. Family members stopped playing the game with him when he began to refer to it as though he were actually living the game and when he became hostile if others joked while playing.

After becoming heavily involved with FRP, Mike Dempsey of Florida became obsessed with the games. His parents notice a definite change in his attitude and outlook. Mike later took his own life.

In June 1982 a sixteen-year-old Virginia boy died as a result of a self-inflicted gunshot wound. His parents told the *Weekly World News* that his death was the result of his involvement with D & D. The boy shot himself just hours after a curse was placed on him by another player.

A teen-ager shoots himself with a sawed-off shotgun in front of his drama class in Arlington, Texas. The youth was a devoted fan of Dungeons & Dragons.

In 1985 two men were charged and convicted in a murder case. The crime was linked to involvement with Dungeons & Dragons.

Daniel E. Erwin, sixteen, and Stephen R. Erwin, twelve, committed suicide as part of a D & D related fantasy.

In reference to the 1985 rape of a young Texas girl, the *Houston Chronicle* on 8 May 1985 reported, "A former prison psychologist and his wife used the fantasy game of Dungeons & Dragons to entice a 15-year-old girl into a sex act. . . ."

Twenty-one-year-old Timothy Grice took his own life in Lafayette, Colorado. Grice apparently believed that he would be able to come back to life as part of the Dungeons & Dragon game.

Three young boys under the age of seventeen were arrested in 1984 for making bombs and poisons and threatening a fellow student with murder. All three boys frequently played D & D.

Eighteen-year-old Lisa Dunn, along with her boyfriend, Danny Rameta, killed four people in Kansas. They were involved in D & D.

Fourteen-year-old Jeffrey Jacklovich stated in his suicide note that he wanted to go to the fantasy world of elves and dwarfs.

Sixteen-year-old Toby Napier was said to be insane when he killed a store clerk in Florida. Napier's attorney said that he "had an obsession with guns, violent movies, paramilitary magazines and the game of Dungeons & Dragons."

A fourteen-year-old boy dies after asking his brother to shoot him in the head to prove that he was invulnerable. The brothers were dedicated players of D & D.

In Ontario, Canada, a twenty-one-year-old male shot and killed thirty-one-year-old Vivian Bremner. The killer, Timothy William Harpur, said he was addicted to computer role-playing games and Dungeons & Dragons and that Bremner was an image in one of those games. "If I didn't kill her I would have lost the game," Harpur said.

The above list could go on for several pages. And yet Dungeons & Dragons is still considered a game, still legally sold in toy and department stores without a warning and still played in and endorsed by some high schools in North America. While Dungeons & Dragons is generally cited as the prime example of potentially dangerous role playing games, it is worth noting that many more FRPs are currently available. Games with fanciful titles, e.g., "Tunnels and Trolls," "Runequest," "The Court of Ardor," and "The Arduin Grimoire" call out to unsuspecting adventure seekers from the shelves of hobby and toy stores.

In her excellent book, *The Devil's Web*, Pat Pulling offers the following useful information regarding those who play Fantasy Role Playing games as well as a list of symptoms which might indicate that an individual has an unhealthy obsession with such games.

**PROFILE OF PARTICIPANTS**

1. Usually very intelligent

2. Creative

3. Ninety-five percent of the players are male with the majority being Caucasian.

4. Imaginative, adventurous

5. Academically interested in history and computer science with a high math aptitude and/or an interest in drama

6. Physically either fairly slight build, clean-cut or possibly overweight and sloppy appearance (generally not the muscular, sports-oriented type)

7. Usually socio-economically from a middle- to upper-middle class family

8. Generally, the adolescent D & D player is not involved with drugs; at most, there may be some use of marijuana. However, if he becomes heavily involved in Satanism, the likelihood of more serious drug use is increased.

9. Adolescents who become heavily involved generally are "good kids" with no prior behavioral problems.

10. The majority of serious players are in the twelve to twenty age group.

11. Manufacturers estimate 4-million-plus active players.

12. Possibly science fiction fan and/or horror film hobbyist

13. Some are loners, but many are not as this is a group-oriented game.

## OBSERVED SYMPTOMS OF OBSESSIVE INVOLVEMENT

1. Loss of interest in other activities

2. Excessive time spent playing fantasy games

3. Drawings depicting cartoon-type figures of gross mutilations, monsters, and/or violent scenes.

4. Drawing occult symbols such as pentagrams, 666, triangles, swastikas, etc.

5. Recurring nightmares

6. Difficulty sleeping, insomnia

7. Change in eating habits

8. Writing poetry with themes of death and dying

9. Written work with themes about supernatural occurrences with dark themes

10. References to a multiplicity of gods
11. Exhibiting a belief in his/her ability to possess psychic powers
12. Speaking in riddles
13. Falling grades
14. Collecting artifacts such as talismans, animal bones, weaponry
15. Fascination with magic, collecting herbs, etc.
16. Threatening to kill others, especially parents
17. Suicidal talk or talking about death; preoccupation with themes of death
18. Deterioration of personal hygiene
19. Hearing voices
20. Obsession with weapons, especially knives
21. Obsession with paramilitary, "Rambo-like" mentality and/or a pre-occupation with war and the violence thereof simply for the sake of the violence
22. Making "pacts" with the devil or, in some cases, suicide pacts[7]

## WHAT'S WRONG WITH A LITTLE MAKE-BELIEVE?

I hope sufficient information has been presented here to establish the fact that Fantasy Role Playing games such as Dungeons & Dragons need to be considered very carefully. But the question still boils down to the basic argument—What's so bad about pretending?

Most people who hold a negative view of FRPs, myself included, are not necessarily against imagination, fantasy, make-believe or pretend. However, we do have a problem with the topics and themes that are presented in these games.

As we have seen, most FRPs are replete with violence, murder, rape, torture, mutilation, and other crimes as well as being steeped in anti-Christian mythology and genuine occult spells, rituals, and doctrines.

As Christians we simply cannot be tolerant of the blasphemous and immoral content of such activities. The

Word of God repeatedly denounces the practices that are promoted by most FRPs and encourages the Christian to think about things that are pure and clean (Phil. 4:8; 1 Thess. 5:21, 22). There simply can be no reason for us to willingly take part in that which God so strongly condemns, whether under the guise of mere fantasy or otherwise.

# 10

# STRICTLY FOR TEEN-AGERS

You are not stupid.

For a long time now, you have been fooling a lot of people into believing that you are ignorant, senseless, unintelligent aliens lacking the common sense of a housefly. Some kids have told me that they do this so that their parents and teachers won't expect too much of them, and they won't be burdened with too much responsibility. But no longer. We're starting to catch on.

Now obviously I am not referring to all young people here. But even if you're considerate, intelligent, well-mannered, etc., please keep reading. I have some thoughts to share with you in a moment as well. But first of all, let's address the kids I mentioned at the beginning. You know who you are. You're the guy who was in great physical condition and used to love playing football, basketball or soccer—but you stopped exercising a long time ago, you don't play sports anymore, and now you drink, smoke, and even do a little grass once in a while.

Deep inside you know you really miss getting that winning touchdown or scoring that tying goal. You feel sluggish and beat all the time, and you wish you had never stopped going to the gym to work out. You couldn't jog a mile now if your life depended on it.

But it's worth it, right? After all, you're cool now—you're one of the crowd. You fit right in with the rest of your friends. Yes, now you're a loser too. Or maybe you're the seventeen-year-old girl who had beautiful golden-blonde hair that reached to your waist just a month ago. You were doing quite well with your classes and everyone thought you'd make it big one day. But you let your friend convince you to cut most of your hair off and to dye the rest an unattractive dark black. You wear ugly clothes now—the worse they look, the more you pretend to like them. You put black eyeliner around your once beautiful, innocent blue eyes, and it makes you look miserable. You party all the time, and you're failing your classes. You no longer let yourself think about your former career plans. You figure you don't stand a chance at it anymore.

It's all worth it, right? After all, you fit right in with your look-alike friends, and they invite you to all of their wonderful parties now too! Aren't you pleased? Now you're a loser just like them! You act like you don't care about yourself or your family or even the world. You act like it's everybody else's fault that no one will hire you or rent you an apartment. But deep inside you know the truth. You know that *you are not stupid* and that you can turn your life around and make some important changes. Deep down inside you think about cleaning up your act. You know you want to. You know you can.

Maybe you're a rough-looking, miserable-acting, totally immature "tough guy." Your friends think you're cool because you never do homework or study for tests, you get lousy grades, and you treat your parents like dirt. You think you're really something special too. You do drugs, smoke and drink, and you act as though you don't love or care about anybody. But deep down inside you wish you were different. You really do care about people. . . . You even love your parents (or at least *like* them). But you know if you show it your "friends" will think you're gutless. You'll lose their respect. Have you ever asked yourself what's more important? Have you ever stopped to consider the fact that guys like the ones you hang around with don't even know the meaning of the word *respect*?

Maybe you've even done the kinds of things we've discussed in this book—foolish things like hurting animals, praying to the devil, desecrating cemeteries, or carving occult symbols on your arms. Maybe you think you are a Satanist.

Chances are, you probably don't even know what a Satanist, really is do you? Do you know why you knock over tombstones or torture cats? Do you know that a *real* Satanist would never do such meaningless things? *Don't you realize you're only fooling yourself and risking the possibility of seriously messing up the rest of your life?*

Oh, but you're different, right? You know when to stop don't you? You are in control, right? Wrong. Countless "tough guys" just like you are in prison right now, some on death row, because they fooled around with something they knew nothing about and had absolutely no control over. Do you really think Sean Sellers woke up one morning and said, "Wouldn't it be great to kill a few people and spend the rest of my life in prison until they decide to execute me?" Are you really dense enough to think that Jim Hardy casually thought to himself, "I think I'll go buy a can of pop and a bag of chips and then go and beat my friend to death with a baseball bat just so they'll lock me up in a penitentiary for the rest of my life."

Wake up! None of the people we've considered in this book (not to mention the others we haven't mentioned) purposely intended to wind up dead or in prison. They all thought that they were tough enough, strong enough, smart enough, or so loved by Satan that nothing could ever go wrong for them. They got involved in something that completely ruined their lives and the lives of their families. What makes you think you're any better? And what about the rock music you listen to? Doesn't it ever bother you that it controls your life, or don't you realize that it does? Isn't it a slap in the face to suddenly wake up and discover that you are a virtual slave to the music? You just can't seem to go without it, can you?

You listen to it when you're driving. You listen to it while you do your homework. You might be one of those kids who can't even go shopping in a mall without your precious earphones and pocket radio. You probably spend a few hours every day just listening to your albums or tapes and you go to concerts whenever you can. You might even be so addicted to music that you can't sleep if it isn't playing all night long.

And how about the hidden messages in rock music? A few years ago people thought that anybody who believed in subliminal messages on rock albums had to be a little crazy. But since then many rock stars have openly admitted putting hidden messages in their music. Doesn't it bother you that your favorite bands might be doing the same thing? Doesn't it bug you to think that your rock-and-roll idols might be messing around with your mind without you even knowing about it? Why are you so devoted to them anyway? Do you think they care about you? Grow up—they don't even know you exist! And if anything ever happened to you, your favorite rock stars wouldn't even notice. Besides, they have thousands and thousands of other fans so why should they care about you?

Several years ago eleven fans were killed at a Who concert in Cincinnati, but did the band care? Apparently not. In fact, Pete Townshend, the guitarist for the Who, told *Rolling Stone* in 1980 that "It was a beneficial experience for the band that they died . . . we don't (expletive deleted) around worrying about eleven dying!"[1] No doubt some of you think that I'm way off here. Maybe you believe that you have complete control over the music rather than the other way around. Well, whether you feel this way or not, I would like to encourage you to accept the following challenge.

In order for you to find out for yourself just how addicted to rock-and-roll you might be, I suggest you stop listening to it for three or four days. That means no cassettes, no albums, no cd's, and no radio. It also means no music videos and no concerts. If you're at a friend's house and he or she has music playing, you leave. If you're out shopping and the store is playing rock music, you leave. If you're at a beach or amusement park and rock music is playing, you leave. If you're at a restaurant and rock music is playing, you leave. This may sound somewhat difficult but keep in mind that it's only for a few days. Actually, this little experiment will benefit you in several ways. In the first place, it will open your eyes to just how widespread rock music really is today. You'll begin to see just how overwhelming it can be when you purposely try to get away from it.

Secondly, depending on your particular lifestyle, you might be amazed when you discover just how much time you waste doing nothing but listening to music.

Third, you might actually find that you are far more relaxed and less hyper when you've gone without rock-and-roll for a few days. Many people are surprised by the noticeable difference. Lastly, and this is the main point of the challenge, you will discover how incredibly addicted to the music you really are. Even people who don't spend a lot of money on albums and never go to concerts are more than a little surprised when they realize how often they listen to rock-and-roll!

If you find that you just can't endure four days without your music, you will begin to understand just how powerful the music really is and how much control it has over you. If this is the case, I sincerely hope and pray that you will begin to take it far more seriously and cautiously and that you will make a concentrated effort to regulate your listening habits and bring them under control.

On the other hand, if you are able to pass this test and go four days without rock-and-roll, why not extend it? Why not make it a day-by-day challenge? Find out if there is a breaking point for you. Can you go six days without rock? seven? ten? With each passing day you will develop a deeper understanding and respect for the awesome power that music can have over people. When you try this experiment, keep in mind that you are an individual, an important, meaningful individual and continually remind yourself that music should be nothing more than entertainment. *It should not control you or your lifestyle.*

If it sounds like I'm coming on a little strong here that's good. I can't help thinking about how my own relatively brief involvement with the occult and Satanism messed up my life and caused tremendous problems between my parents and myself. I can't forget how very close I came to taking my own life one night because I thought it was the only possible way to end my involvement with the devil when, in reality, committing suicide would have been the worst thing I could have done. I can't help thinking about where I'd be today, or even if I'd still be alive if I hadn't made the decision to end my involvement with Satanism when I did.

Teen-ager, no matter who you are, where you are, what you look like, or what kind of things you're into right now, I want you to know something.

I want you to know that you are the whole reason behind this book. You are why I wrote this book. You are why I spent untold hours typing and changing and correcting and adding and subtracting. You are the reason I went through numerous hassles and problems trying to get this book written. You are the reason that I studied and researched and learned all I could about the problem of Satanism among young people today.

I want you to know that regardless of what you might think or what you might have been told, I really care about you. . . . And so do a lot of other people—more people than you can imagine.

I want you to know that Satan is a liar and he's been lying to you since day one. There really is a way for you to turn your life around. There really are people who will do whatever they can to help you get your life together.

There really is hope. And there really is a way to be free from the terrible bondage you are experiencing. I want you to know that you are special. You are unique. And your life really is worth something! You need to understand that it doesn't take any courage to do what all your friends are doing. It doesn't take strength to fit in with the crowd, to smoke because everyone else smokes, to drink because everyone else drinks, to do drugs because everyone else does drugs, or to mess with Satanism because your friends are.

Do you want to know what really does take strength, what really requires courage? If you really want to show how strong you are, how brave you are, or if you really want to show that you are in control of your life, I challenge you to consider becoming a follower of Jesus Christ. Now that takes guts!

A lot of kids seem to think that you have to be a sissy to be a Christian. Far from it! Like I said, it takes guts to be different—to stand up for what you believe in even when your friends are all doing the opposite. Actually, if they just took the time to read the New Testament and think about it a little bit, they'd soon realize that Christians are anything but weak, trembling sissies.

Consider the Apostle Paul. He was beaten numerous times, thrown into prison repeatedly, he received thirty-nine lashes (whippings) five different times, was beaten with rods three times, shipwrecked three times and more! (see 2 Cor. 11:23-27).

James was executed by the sword (Acts 12:1, 2). John the baptist was beheaded (Mark 6:16-29). Peter was imprisoned (Acts 12:3-5). Stephen was murdered by an angry crowd that threw stones and rocks at him until he died (Acts 7:57-60). And hundreds of thousands of Christians through the ages have suffered unbelievable tortures and deaths because they had the courage to stand up for what they believed in (Heb. 11:32-40).

And what about Jesus Christ Himself? Jesus was

rejected by His own people. He was constantly ridiculed and criticized. Eventually He was arrested, flogged, and finally crucified. Yet He could have delivered Himself from His captors anytime He wanted (John 1:10-12; 19:1-3, 17-37; Matt. 26:50-54). But He didn't. He didn't because He had the courage and strength to stand up for what He believed in and to do what He knew He had to do. So consider it my friend—do you have the guts to follow Jesus and become a Christian or are you going to waste your life by constantly trying to fit in with the crowd?

**JESUS WANTS TO HELP YOU!**

If you are involved in the occult you may be fearful of trying to escape it. I know I was! The night I finally gave in and cried out to the Lord to save me, I truly believed with all my heart that the devil himself was going to come into my room during the night and kill me. Instead, I enjoyed the best night of sleep that I have ever had and I awoke the next morning eager and excited about starting my first day as a new creation in Jesus Christ! (see 2 Cor. 5:17).

Although I had been afraid of Satan because I thought he was stronger than God, I soon came across all kinds of Scripture passages that told me the truth about the matter. I've listed some of my favorites for you. Maybe they'll become special to you too.

"Behold, I have given you authority to tread upon serpents and scorpions, *and overall the power of the enemy,* and nothing shall injure you. Nevertheless do not rejoice in this, that the spirits are subject to you, but rejoice that your names are recorded in heaven"(Luke 10:19, 20 italics mine).

". . . . The Son of God (Jesus) appeared for this purpose, *that He might destroy the works of the devil*" (1 John 3:8 italics and brackets added).

"You are from God, little children, and have overcome them; because *greater is He (Jesus) who is in you* than he (Satan) who is in the world"(1 John 4:4 italics and brackets added).

"Submit therefore to God. Resist the devil *and he will flee from you*"( James 4:7 italics and brackets added).

Now don't get me wrong. I'm not saying it's necessarily going to be easy for you to leave your involvement with the occult or Satanism and become a Christian. In fact, depending on how deeply you are involved, it may be a very difficult and possibly dangerous endeavor. However, at the end of this book, I have included a listing of several organizations that are very experienced in helping people who are in situations like yours.

I encourage you to contact these organizations right away so that you can begin to sever your ties with Satan as soon as possible.

**FIRST THINGS FIRST**

The very first thing you need to do however is to invite the Lord Jesus into your heart and life and repent of your sins. In fact, you need to do this regardless of whether or not you have ever been involved in Satanism! Jesus Himself said that *everyone* must be born-again in order to get into heaven (see John 3:3; 3:5; & 3:7).

Accepting Jesus as Saviour and Lord is far easier than you might think. It does not cost any money. It does not require that you join any club or organization or even a church. And it certainly does not require that you break any laws (as some satanic initiations do).

The first step is to recognize that you are a sinner in need of a Saviour. The Bible teaches that everyone has sinned in one way or another and fallen short of God's glory (Rom. 3:10; 3:23). Secondly, ask the Lord to forgive all of your past sins (you might feel better if you actually list any sins that stand out in your mind and cause you to feel guilty) and to wash away your sins with the precious blood, which He shed on the cross.

Next, invite the Lord into your heart and life and ask Him to help you live for Him. You might pray something like this, "Dear Lord, I know I am a sinner. I also know that You are the only one who can forgive my sins and wash them away. Please forgive me for all that I have done wrong in my life. Please come into my life and accept me into the family of God. I accept You now as my Lord and Saviour, and I ask that You help me to live the way You want me to live from this day forward. Amen." Now if you said that prayer and meant it with all your heart (it's important to be sincere, you can't fool God!), you are now a brand new, born-again believer! (see John 6:37).

In order to properly grow in your new faith it is extremely important that you read the Bible everyday. You should stay in the New Testament for a few months before getting into the Old Testament and be sure to pray each time before you read. Ask the Lord to help you to understand His Word and to grow in your walk with Him. Also, it is very important to find a solid, Bible-believing church to attend so that you will be able to learn and have the support of other Christians.

Remember to contact any of the organizations listed at the end of this book if you have any questions or if you want additional information on the Bible or Christianity. If you'd like, you may write to me at the address below. We'd love to hear from you!

Victory Through Jesus Ministries
P.O. Box 503
Niagara Falls, Ontario
Canada L2E 6V2

Welcome to your new life in Christ!

## RECOMMENDED READING

The Holy Bible

# 11

# CHRIST'S RETURN & THE POPULARITY OF THE OCCULT

"But the Spirit explicitly says that in latter times some will fall away from the faith, paying attention to deceitful spirits and doctrines of demons" (1 Tim. 4:1). There is no doubt in my mind that the current occult and New Age craze is a direct fulfillment of biblical prophecy. Many other Scripture passages combine to warn of an approaching time, just prior to Christ's return, when men will knowingly and willingly worship demons. Peter Lalonde, well-known prophecy speaker and publisher of the *Omega Letter*, says, "What we are seeing today is a realization, or at the very least, the first steps toward the realization, of Revelation 13:4. The unheard of is beginning to happen—people are literally bending the knee to Satan himself. The stage is being set for worldwide worship of the Devil and his antichrist."

Thousands of teen-agers are wearing T-shirts that blatantly glorify Satan and demons. The 666 is a common emblem on jackets. Music that openly and clearly praises the devil and presents him as an unfortunate, misunderstood being is becoming more prevalent. The Apostle Paul provides additional words of warning in 2 Timothy where he writes about the "perilous times" that will come. Even a casual rumination of the traits listed by Paul as characterizing the last days, causes one to believe that his words are coming to pass in the 90s. He writes of men being lovers of self, lovers of money, boastful, arrogant, revilers, disobedient to parents, ungrateful, unholy, unloving, irreconcilable, malicious gossips, without self control, brutal, haters of good, treacherous, reckless, conceited, lovers of pleasure rather than lovers of God.

A more accurate description of mankind in this present day could not have been written if the Apostle was actually on the earth today! Several of the traits mentioned are in line with what we have been considering throughout this book.

**Lovers of money**: Money is everything today, and this materialistic philosophy is constantly promoted by the extravagant lifestyles of rock musicians and movie stars who pose as heroes and idols to millions of teen-agers throughout the world.

**Arrogant**: Kids today seem to feel they don't need anybody. They don't need their parents or teachers and they don't need God or the church. They are defiant and untouchable.

**Revilers**: This word could be *the* word to describe teen-agers today, particularly since dictionary definitions of the word make mention of "abusive language." Kids today are cursing and swearing at an early age, and it sometimes seems that some of them are incapable of speaking without throwing in the *F*-word from time to time.

**Disobedient to parents**: If *revilers* is the word to describe teens today, then *disobedient to parents* is "the phrase." There is no question that parents have lost the authority they once had and no longer receive the respect from their teen-agers that they are due. Of course, neither do the police, school teachers, etc.

**Ungrateful**: Parents work hard for years to provide for their kids. They give-up many of their own dreams and desires for the sake of their kids. But when kids get messed up with heavy metal or black metal rock, they progress to drug or alcohol use, and possibly get into Satanism or the occult. These kids quickly forget about their parents. Of course, what can we expect when some popular rock bands publicly promote rebellion against parents and society. Not to mention the fact that Satanism is a very selfish religion where no one else matters, not even mom and dad.

**Unholy**: An awful lot of teen-agers (as well as adults) would certainly fit into this category. An alarming number of kids have no respect or reverence for God. They feel that religion is useless and that the Church is made up of phonies and hypocrites. The lifestyle so popular with kids today is anything but holy.

**Lovers of pleasure rather than lovers of God**: This one doesn't really need any explaining! The prevailing attitude of North Americans is clearly, "Live for today!" Our society is obsessed with a "buy-now-pay-later" mentality, which obviously carries over into other areas of day-to-day living. In fact, it is this "I'll worry about it later" syndrome that is causing so many kids to delve into drugs, alcohol, the occult, and other questionable practices without a second thought. When confronted with the prospect of eternal damnation many kids laugh it off and say they'll worry about crossing that bridge when they get to it. Unfortunately, it won't be that easy. The Bible declares that today (not next week) is the day of salvation (2 Cor. 6:2). But Satan has them convinced that there's nothing more important than having a good time.

We could go on with this analysis but I trust I've made my point. That which the Bible predicts for the last days before the return of the Lord Jesus Christ is happening before our very eyes. And the growing problem of Satanism among young people is a very definite part of it.

## BUT WORSHIP A BEAST?

We have already considered the main reasons why kids are choosing to involve themselves with Satanism and the occult. But let's take this opportunity to look at it another way.

Thousands of people, perhaps millions, are actually and literally worshipping the devil. It's difficult to fathom, but they actually admire him!

Some kids think he's the greatest. Possibly because, like them, Satan is different, unconventional. But they also love him because with Satan, anything goes.

Let's face it, Satan offers people what they want. Do you want to flirt with every member of the opposite sex you meet? Do you want to lie to your friends just to make a quick buck? Do you want to waste your whole paycheck on drugs or booze and get high every night? If you're a Satanist, all of this is permitted—all of this, and more! There simply are no rules.

A popular phrase among Satanists sums this up concisely, "Do what thou wilt shall be the whole of the law."

Satan is so successful at reaping souls because anyone who follows him can do whatever he or she pleases. In fact, they are encouraged to enjoy this life. His followers are encouraged to get out and party until they drop, to drink and smoke, to swear, and lust, and lie. The fact that they are allowed to live as they wish and not be questioned about it turns a lot of people (especially young people) on to following Satan.

But did you catch the proverbial fine print there? He promises to provide you with what you want *for this life.* He doesn't discuss what will happen to you on the day of judgment (Rev. 20:11-12). In fact, by the time his followers realize what they're in for, they're usually too caught up in the pleasures of this world to really care.

Satan approaches young people with his lies and deceit with lines of reasoning like, "Look, what do you want? A night of fun with that great looking blonde or another boring night at home reading the Bible?" Given the choice, an awful lot of kids answer with, "I want to spend the night with the blonde, of course!"

The devil constantly uses this type of trick—"You only live once" or "Life is short" or "You won't be here forever so grab everything you can!" When you hear someone talking like this, you can rest assured that Satan has conditioned that person to feel this way.

To illustrate this in a down-to-earth manner, let's assume that I was to offer you one thousand dollars now or ten thousand dollars if you waited twenty years. Now think about these choices and decide which one you would pick. Keep in mind that the majority of devil-may-care, partying teen-agers tend to be interested in the here and now and don't give a lot of thought to their distant future. So, Satan offers people whatever they want for this life while God offers us much more but not until later. This way, countless people who want carnal pleasures and riches now, accept the devil's offer even though much greater rewards could have been theirs. The saddest part of this is that although the Lord offers us so many grand and glorious rewards in eternity, we're forgetting to tell the kids that He has plenty to offer right now as well!

We're forgetting to tell them about the happiness that belonging to Jesus can bring. We're forgetting to tell them about the hope He gives us, the reason for living. And perhaps most of all, we're forgetting to let them know about the wonderful peace that Jesus gives even in the midst of a crazy, mixed-up world. The kids need to hear these things. The Bible clearly indicates that people will miss the blessings of the Lord because they are not willing to give up their earthly pleasures (Mark 10:17-23). No doubt many of you who have witnessed for Christ have come up against people caught in this mind set. So many people feel that the so-called pleasures of this world are too much to give up. The Lord spoke strongly about this type of attitude in Matthew 6:33, "But seek first His kingdom and His righteousness; and all these things shall be added to you" (see also Rom. 12:2; James 4:4; 1 John 2:15).

Sometimes we find ourselves face-to-face with a person who takes this excuse even further by constantly trying to "better himself" in this world—making more and more money, buying better homes and cars, constantly trying to obtain more and more. This type of person is usually difficult to reach with the Gospel because he has let money and material possessions become more important than anything else—even eternity. Those who are buying into Satan's temptations to allow the "finer things of life" to outweigh their concern for their spiritual condition would do well to consider the Lord's words, "For what does it profit a man to gain the whole world and forfeit his soul? For what shall a man give in exchange for his soul?" (Mark 8:36-37).

As we draw nearer and nearer to the return of the Lord, we see a widespread love of money and possessions. It seems that with every passing day people are caring less and less about the things of the Lord. And yet, with the terrible condition the world is in—economic problems, extreme human suffering, deadly pollution—we should be doing the opposite—we should be calling out to God and falling on our faces before Him.

This brings us right back to where we began. When the Antichrist comes on the scene offering answers to all the world's problems, arranging peace throughout the planet, repairing the economy, who he is and what his motives are won't matter in the least. People will be so relieved to see his wonderful works that it won't matter that he gets his powers and abilities from Satan himself. And what about those who worship him? What about the countless kids who we've considered throughout this book—the kids who think that the devil is the greatest? What about adults throughout the world who actively worship demons and promote a satanic religion? Naturally, such people will fall at his feet believing that their redeemer, their saviour, has arrived. They will welcome him with open arms just like the Word of God predicts.

But later the enemy will show his true colors. It is then that these people will realize, to their horror, that they have been terribly deceived. It is then that they will realize that it is literally and completely impossible for the devil to love or care about *anyone*. That is precisely why we need to work harder *now*. We need to reach these kids with the truth of the Gospel and the love of Jesus Christ *before* it's too late. We need to stop fussing and fighting about the minor details, the differences of opinions regarding clothing styles, haircuts, and musical tastes and start concentrating on what really counts—the salvation of souls.

# APPENDIX A

# WHY SACRIFICE?

One of the first things that comes to mind when we hear the word *Satanism* is an unholy ceremony involving a human or animal sacrifice.

The world was stunned just a few years ago when the remains of several unfortunate victims were discovered at Matamoros, Mexico. These people had been sacrificed in ceremonies involving a weird blend of Palo Mayombe (Voodoo) and Satanism.

Unfortunately, it would seem that many people have already forgotten the sickening tragedy of Matamoros. I frequently meet such people who are once again burying their heads in the sand and insisting that such things as human sacrifice "simply don't happen."

**BUT IT *DOES* HAPPEN**

While it is difficult to prove or support numerically, many experts believe such sacrifices do take place several times every year in accordance with satanic, high "holy" days. Furthermore, these experts contend that many individuals have been ritualistically sacrificed by dabblers or self-styled Satanists. As was noted earlier however, such sacrifices are usually made in a vain attempt to appear satanic. In actual fact, the murderer in such cases has no real concept as to why sacrifices are carried out nor does he know the proper manner in which to do so.

Regardless of such inconsequential aspects, the question one generally asks after hearing about ritual sacrifice is, *Why*? Basically, human or animal sacrifices take place for three reasons. First of all, sacrifices are offered as gifts to please certain occult deities or demons. This reasoning is evident in numerous cultural beliefs including some North American Indian tribes, ancient Aztecs, and various African tribes. The logic is that if the gods are kept placated with gifts (sacrifices), they will not harm the tribe, village, etc. Secondly, sacrifices are used in satanic and black magic circles for the purpose of harnessing the energy of the victim when it is released (at the moment of death) and using said energy for magical purposes.

There are two schools of thought concerning such sacrifice. One school believes that the victim, be it animal or human, should be mercilessly tortured for extended periods before actually being killed. This is done so that the fear and emotions of the victim are pushed higher and higher until they reach "fever pitch" at the point of death. The other, more traditional view, holds that the death should be as swift as possible (i.e., one well-aimed stab to a vital area rather than several "hit-and-miss" blows). The reasoning for this is that the desired energy of the victim will be released in one powerful rush as opposed to slipping away slowly as it would during torture. It should be noted that sexual rituals are based on the same principles with the magician attempting to harness the energy that is released at the point of orgasm. Of the two, rituals involving sacrifice are held to be more powerful since virtually all of the victim's energy is released at the point of death.

Thirdly, sacrifice, or more accurately the fear of sacrifice, is used as a method of controlling other cult members or outsiders. Those found to be disloyal to the group or anyone considering leaving the cult could be used as the next sacrificial victim. Of course, those involved in such situations would fear, not only the ritual itself, but would also greatly fear what their "lord" Satan would have in store for their souls.

## WHO ARE THE VICTIMS?

While it is almost impossible to substantiate, women have come forward over the past few years and claimed to have given birth for the purpose of sacrifice. This practice is known as "breeding," and it holds several advantages for the Satanists. In the first place, any babies born within the group, without the aid of hospitals or doctors, would be unknown. The state would not even know that such babies existed. Therefore, it is a simple matter to have the baby, sacrifice the baby, and bury the baby without anyone "on the outside" having any knowledge of it. There would be no birth certificates, no social security numbers issued, no hospital records, and no death certificates—the perfect crime?

In addition to this, sacrifice victims can be lone hitchhikers picked up on some deserted stretch of highway, never to be heard from again. Or they could be young runaways, prostitutes, or drunks—people that society doesn't seem to care much about and certainly wouldn't miss as much as a politician or television star. Many cult researchers, myself included, tend to believe that at least some of the countless young people that are reported missing every year end up as human sacrifices.

As mentioned above, some sacrifice victims may be members of the particular group who have fallen out of favor with the leader for one reason or another. It is also possible that members might actually volunteer to be sacrificed on rare occasions with the hope of pleasing their master. It is my hope that the general public, whether Christian or otherwise, will begin to wake up to the horrible realities of Satanism and the occult as more and more reports of ritualistic crime begin to surface.

# APPENDIX B

# SUICIDE: A POSSIBLE RESULT OF OCCULT INVOLVEMENT

In earlier chapters of this book we have seen how some kids become so discouraged with life that death seems like the only answer. We have considered those who become so wrapped up in the black arts or Satanism that they become literally obsessed with death and dying. We have also considered those who are influenced by blatantly fatalistic lyrics in some rock music—music that actually encourages the listener to kill himself/herself. And we have looked at some unfortunate instances of suicide that were linked to Fantasy Role Playing games like Dungeons & Dragons. After considering such information, I would be remiss not to include this section on suicide.

The Centers for Disease Control in Atlanta, Georgia, say that as many as half a million suicide attempts take place every year with as many as five thousand resulting in death. Certainly the problem of suicide is nothing new. However, given the additional pressures of life in the 90s combined with the previously mentioned considerations, it is a problem that deserves our attention. If you have noticed in your child any of the warning signs of possible occult involvement outlined in this book, you should also keep your eyes open to warning signs of a possible suicide attempt.

**WARNING SIGNS OF SUICIDE**

*Death, blood, graves, suicide, etc., are all important

aspects of Satanism and the black arts. If your child starts referring to such topics on a regular or frequent basis, pay attention. Certainly a child or teen-ager threatening to commit suicide might just be trying to shock people or get his/her own way. However, it simply isn't worth taking the chance. If threats of suicide start to surface, consult a professional. Don't gamble with your child's life!

*Drug or alcohol abuse might indicate a teen-ager who no longer cares whether he lives or dies.

*Mood swings, personality changes, fits of rage or anger might indicate that the individual is seriously considering a major decision (whether or not to kill himself). Teen-agers naturally go through spells like this simply because of the many changes they are going through and the new pressures they feel as they get older. However, any such mood or personality changes that continue for extended periods should be considered carefully. This is particularly true if there doesn't appear to be any reason for such moodiness.

*Changes in activities, particularly if the individual suddenly stops doing things that once gave him great pleasure, could indicate a problem. This is especially important if a once outgoing and energetic individual suddenly becomes moody and listless. This could indicate a "what's the use" or "life isn't worth living" attitude.

*Eating or sleeping habits might change if a person is considering suicide. Someone who is serious about ending his life certainly won't care if he's getting enough sleep or eating the right foods.

*Neglecting personal appearance or hygiene is a telltale sign as well. While appearance is extremely important to most young people today, if someone is planning on committing suicide, chances are their appearance will be the last thing on their mind.

*Difficulty in concentrating, a sudden or drastic drop in grades, or constant boredom could be an indication that something is weighing heavily on your teen-ager's mind.

*Being careless, accident prone, or taking senseless risks might display an attitude of indifference. Again, someone intent on taking his own life won't be overly concerned about safety.

*Anyone who has previously attempted suicide should be taken that much more seriously if he mentions suicide again. He's already shown that he has the effrontery to try it and might be completely serious.

*Discomfort with praise or compliments. In many cases a person decides to commit suicide because he or she feels totally useless and unlovable. Having reached that conclusion, your compliments will be difficult to accept.

*Frequent complaints regarding ailments that are associated with emotions (e.g., headaches, stomachaches, tiredness, etc.) should cause you to keep a close watch on your teen-ager.

*Distributing prized possessions, giving personal items away, or attempting to clear up past misunderstandings with others could indicate that an individual isn't planning on hanging around too much longer. Don't ignore such obvious clues.

Naturally, a delicate balance is called for in such serious matters. On the one hand, you don't want to become paranoid and call 911 every time your teen-ager seems down or upset. But then, you don't want to wait till it's too late before you decide to take action either.

As I've tried to stress throughout this book, the best thing you, as a parent or concerned adult, can do is just get involved. Take an active interest in your kids. Let them know, not just by words but by actions, that you are there for them. Let them know that you care about them. Let them know that they can come to you regardless of what they've done, regardless of how they may feel.

Chances are, if we begin to take steps to be friends and allies with kids today, we won't need to be as concerned about them hurting themselves or others.

# Appendix C

# OUIJA BOARDS AND OTHER OCCULT TOYS

It goes without saying that occult involvement generally involves the traditional trappings of spiritism, seances, Ouija boards, table rapping, automatic writing, and so on. Because such popular practices can often lead to a deeper involvement in the occult, a brief consideration and explanation of such activities is provided here.

## OUIJA BOARDS

Often pronounced "Wee-gee," the name of this spiritism device is actually derived from the French word for "yes," *oui*, and the German word for "yes," *ja*. Therefore, the Ouija board is actually the "yes-yes board" and is properly pronounced "Wee-jah." The Ouija board, or more accurately, devices *like* the Ouija board, has been around for centuries and can be traced to ancient civilizations in various parts of the world. The "board" is any flat, smooth surface with letters, numbers, symbols, or words on it. A drinking glass or other object is used as a pointer to spell out different words or phrases.

The Ouija works best when two (as opposed to one) individuals are involved. Each participant places his/her fingers lightly on the glass, more properly called the planchette, and concentrates while one participant asks questions of the board.

If the spirits are in a talkative mood at the time, the planchette will begin to move across the board and point to various letters in order to spell out its responses. It is interesting to note that experiments have been conducted with the board whereby the participants were blindfolded and the letters on the board scrambled. Yet the planchette still pointed to letters and correctly spelled out answers to various questions.* Such results suggest the possibility that there is more than the subconscious mind of the players at work.

So where does Ouija get its answers? From the spirits of friends and relatives who have passed away? From intelligent entities from a different plane, perhaps? Or from demonic spirits? Certainly there can be no empirical response to such queries, and opinions on the topic are divided. However, one thing is certain—there would appear to be far more reasons to stay away from the Ouija than there are to use it.

There are those who claim to have been flung from their chairs while "playing" the Ouija. Others seem to have opened the door to the spirit world and are relentlessly plagued by disturbing occurrences thereafter. Still others report witnessing unleashed fury when asking the board about the Lord Jesus Christ or the power of His blood.

It is noteworthy indeed that the most outspoken group to warn against the Ouija is not the fundamental Christians as one might expect, but the spiritists themselves! Many people involved in spiritism are quick to point out that the Ouija is not a game and that it is better left alone. In 1920 the IRS declared that the Ouija board was a game and therefore its sales should be taxable. The court agreed with the IRS, and from then on, this ancient spiritualist device has been considered nothing more than a parlor game.

* William Barrett, *On the Threshhold of the Unseen* (New York: Dutton, 1918), 181.

## TAROT CARDS

Tarot (pronounced "tar-o") cards consist of the Major Arcanum (twenty cards) and the Minor Arcanum (fifty-six cards). The cards are a type of fortune-telling device based on the theory that every occurrence is the result of casual laws. Naturally, for the tarot to work, we must also assume that there is no such thing as haphazard chance in any degree.

## ASTRAL PROJECTION

Also known as Soul Travel. This is the practice of separating the so-called astral body from the physical body in order to travel to places that would be otherwise unreachable. Astral projection is commonly tried by teen-agers when they are beginning their interest in the occult or Satanism. Many people claim that they have been able to describe the interior of locked rooms or the activities of people within such rooms by supposedly projecting themselves inside.

Whether or not this is possible or merely another deception of the enemy cannot be proven to the satisfaction of all. However, it should be mentioned that many people have reported experiencing such terror while practiscing soul travel that they refuse to ever try it again.

## AUTOMATIC WRITING

Automatic writing is the phenomena involving involuntary drawing or writing by an individual. Some people have developed automatic writing abilities after using the Ouija board. Some interesting facts about automatic writing include:

*Writing is often completely different from the actual handwriting of the participant.

*Entire books written by automatic writing.

*Both hands are sometimes involved with both hands writing in a completely different style and about completely different topics at the same time.*

* Stoker Hunt, *Ouija: The Most Dangerous Game* (New York: Harper and Row, Inc., 1985), 16, 130.

*Automatic writing has been done while the participant is blindfolded and unable to see the boundaries of the page or the words he/she is wrlting.

*Automatic writing is sometimes done backwards necessitating the use of a mirror to read the finished work.

## WHO WROTE THIS?

It is a chilling thought indeed when one considers the possibility of reading a novel or a poem or song lyrics which may have been written by a non-human entity.

What of the various volumes on black magic or satanic magic. Could it not be possible that such ancient secrets were penned by someone or something other than a human? And what about those absolutely chilling horror novels or movies, the kind that make you shake your head and ask, "Where do these ideas come from?"

And of course, what about those oh-so-controversial rock lyrics. Some artists have admitted that on occasion they have sat down and penned songs that have gone on to be tremendous hits, without ever giving it any thought or effort. Certainly something to think about!

## MIRROR GAZING

This is the occult practice of staring into a mirror for extended periods of time. Doing so is supposed to reveal various secrets or information to the practitioner, however, there are reports of people going insane as a result of mirror gazing.* Obviously, when one stares at an object, any object, for great lengths of time, it is only natural that one would begin to "see things."

Crystals and the surface of still water are used in the same way and for the same purposes. Mirror gazing is another practice that is frequently tried by young people with little or no knowledge of the occult. It is not something to toy with.

## PSYCHOMETRY

Psychometry is the ability to "read" information from

* F.W. Thomas, *Kingdom of Darkness* (Plainfield, NJ: Logos Internatioaal, 1973), 74-75.

inanimate objects. To do so, the "reader" holds a personal belonging such as an item of clothing, a wallet, etc., and is able to describe various traits of the owner of said item. In some cases the medium is able to describe past or future events in the life of the owner of the item.

## TEA LEAF READING

Also referred to as Teacup reading, this is yet another form of divination. The reader attempts to interpret the shapes and forms of tea leaves as they settle on the bottom of the cup.

## PALMISTRY

Commonly called palm reading, this ancient occult method of divining attempts to forecast one's future by reading the various lines and markings found in the palm of the hand.

## ASTROLOGY

Astrologists would have us believe that the position of the various stars and planets directly influence our lives. Therefore, our future can be predicted by determining the position of the stars and planets at the time of our birth. Scientific discoveries with regards to our solar system have largely disproved any validity of the practice. However, millions of people continue to live their lives based entirely on what their daily horoscopes tell them.

Horoscopes are found in thousands of daily newspapers, countless magazines, booklets, and are even available by dialing special advertised telephone numbers that offer recorded horoscopes.

## SEANCES

Seances involve a group of people attempting to contact the spirits of the dead. This is another activity that is frequently looked upon as harmless party fun. Most people, however, have never given any serious consideration to the important question, "What will I do *if we do contact something?*"

## CHANNELLING

This refers to the dangerous practice of temporarily

giving up control of one's cognitive and perceptual faculties to a spiritual entity in order to obtain information from said entity. Channelling is basically the New Age name for the similar practice of mediumship.

## CRYSTALS

New Agers claim that crystals possess extraordinary powers that can be used for healing or other positive endeavors. Crystals are also supposed to be useful in restoring one's "energy flow." Personally, I believe that these wonderful, amazing, powerful, miraculous crystals are really something else—pretty rocks and nothing more.

## PSYCHOKINESIS

Also known as telekinesis, this is the practice of causing objects to move without physically touching them.

The above list is by no means to be considered exhaustive. It is my hope, however, that the reader has been provided with a basic understanding as to what some of the more popular occult practices are all about. In closing, I should point out that many adults (parents) tend to read their horoscopes in the daily newspaper and might even go to fortune tellers "just for fun." I even know of a Christian pastor who claims there is nothing at all wrong with reading horoscopes!

Please let me take this opportunity to remind you that you will be far less effective in trying to warn teen-agers away from the occult if you are partaking in it yourself. Besides, there is absolutely no good reason why a Christian should so much as glance at a horoscope or visit a fortune teller.

The Word of God is replete with stern warnings and admonitions against occult involvement of any kind (see Ex. 22:18; Lev. 19:31; Duet. 18:10-12; 2 Chron. 33:6; Mic. 5:12; etc).

# Appendix D

# A BIBLICAL VIEW OF SATAN & HIS DEMONS

The Bible contains many references to the existence of a personality of extreme evilness. This being is commonly referred to as Satan or the devil, but he has many different names and titles some of which are: Great Dragon (Rev. 12:9); Prince of this World (John 12:31); Prince of the Power of the Air (Eph. 2:2); Serpent (Rev. 12:9); God of this Age (2 Cor. 4:4); Murderer (John 8:44); Liar (John 8:44); Prince of demons (Luke 11:15 ); the Enemy (Matt. 13:39); Satan (Zech. 3:1; Rev. 12:9); Belial (2 Cor. 6:15); Devil (Luke 4:2; Rev. 12:9); the Evil One (John 17:15); Destroyer (Rev. 9:11); Deceiver (Rev. 12:9; 20:3); Adversary (Zech. 3:1); Wicked One (Matt. 6:13; 13:19); Accuser (Matt. 13:39; John 8:44); and Tempter (Gen. 3; Matt. 4:1-11).

Satan is the greatest enemy of God and man. His existence is set forth as fact in the Scriptures (Matt. 13:19 & 39; John 13:2; Acts 5:3; 2 Cor. 11:3 & 14; 2 Peter 2:24; etc.). He is referred to in seven books of the Old Testament and mentioned by name in nineteen of the twenty-seven books of the New Testament. In addition to this, four of the remaining eight books mention demons and/or evil angels. We find twenty-nine references to Satan in the four Gospel books, twenty-five of which are made by Christ.

The Bible teaches that Satan was originally a beautiful and wise angel named Lucifer. However, Lucifer's pride and arrogance led to his fall from heaven. This fall was probably in connection with the fall of the angels, which is also recorded in Scripture (see Ez. 28:12-19; Is. 14:12-14; John 8:44; Luke 10:18; 2 Peter 2:4; Jude 6; 1 Tim. 3:6; Matt. 25:41; 2 Cor. 11:14; etc.). It is important to realize that there is no biblical basis for representing Satan as a theatre-type monster with horns, hooves, tail, and sharply pointed pitchfork.

The Word of God makes it clear that Satan is the epitome of evil. He is described within Scripture as a murderer, liar, thief, accuser, and so on (see John 8:44; 1 John 3:8; etc.). Furthermore, Satan is plainly described as a personal being. Personal pronouns are applied to him in Scripture as well as personal characteristics and actions. He possesses attributes of personality and is pictured as male (or masculine). The temptation of Jesus in the wilderness is but one forthright example of Satan set forth as a person (see also Job 1 & 2; Zech. 3:1-2; 1 Chron. 21:1; Psalm 109:6; Matt. 4:1- 11; etc.).

It should also be noted that Christ spoke of the existence of Satan as a fact while He was on the earth.

## THE PLACE AND POWER OF SATAN

Satan is truly a powerful being and not simply a little "imp" to be toyed with (Jude 8-9; Dan. 10:12-13; Luke 11:21). The Bible also alludes to the fact that the world of Satan and the fallen angels is organized and that it has tremendous power over this world (see Eph. 2:1-2; 6:11-12; Matt. 9:34; 12:24; Luke 11:14-18; 2 Cor. 4:4; John 12:31; 14:30; 16:11; 1 John 5:19; etc).

The devil is presented as the leader of a kingdom of his own which is completely opposed to the Kingdom of God (Acts 26:18; Col. 1:13). And, far from being weak and harmless, it is written that Satan has sovereignty over the realm of death (Heb. 2:14). Although, this is not to imply that he has the authority to indiscriminately murder God's people.

Some of the items listed as "Satan's work" by Emery H. Bancroft include, originated sin, causes suffering, causes death, allures to evil, ensnares men, inspires wicked thoughts and purposes, takes possession of men, blinds the minds of men, dissipates the truth, produces a fruitage of evil doers, energizes his ministers, opposes God's servants, tests believers, accuses believers, and he will energize the Antichrist.*

## OUR ATTITUDE TOWARD SATAN

Although Satan is strong, it is imperative that the believer realize that his power against the child of God is limited. He is not almighty (Job 1:9-12; 2:4-6; John 12:31; 16:11). This is not to say that he should be totally ignored, for the Bible clearly admonishes us to resist him (1 Peter 5:8-9; James 4:7). The only way to effectively resist the enemy is to be submitted to the Lord and equipped with the whole armor of God (Rom. 6:17- 23; James 4:7; Eph. 6:10-20).

## THE DESTINY OF SATAN

First and foremost, Satan is already defeated, but only so far as the believer is concerned (John 12:31; 16:9-10; Col. 2:15; 1 John 3:8). Unlike men, Satan has no chance for redemption (Gen. 3:14; Is. 65:25). When all is said and done, Satan will be cast into the Lake of Fire to be tormented day and night forever (Matt. 25:41; Rev. 20:10).

## DEMONS

The origin of demons is not specifically expressed in the Bible. Some believe that they are one in the same with the fallen angels (Matt. 25:41; Rev. 12:7-9) but are not to be confused with those fallen angels presently bound and awaiting judgment (2 Pet. 2:4; Jude 6). It is evident however, that Satan is their ruler (Matt. 12:22-28; Eph. 6:12).

Demons are totally evil and are able to possess the bodies of men and women (Matt. 10:1; Mark 5:1-13). They can be cast out in the name of Jesus (Acts 16:18). They, too, have no chance of redemption.

*Emery H. Bancroft. *Elemental Theology*. Zondervan Publishers, Grand Rapids, Mich., 1977. pp. 331-334.

The biblical record suggests that demons are able to inflict humans with various physical ailments such as deafness, blindness, dumbness, etc. (Matt. 12:22-23).

Demons are also referred to as seducing spirits (1 Tim. 4:1), unclean spirits (Mark 1:27), evil spirits (Luke 7:21), and familiar spirits (Lev. 20:6).

Demons will be busy in these last days deluding men and taking part in Armageddon (1 Tim. 4:1; Rev. 16:13-16).

# Appendix E

# A BIBLE STUDY ON THE TOPIC OF SATAN & DEMONS

1. What was the devil's name before he fell from heaven? ______________________________

2. Why did he fall from heaven? ______________

______________________________________________

______________________________________________

______________________________________________

3. Ezekiel tells us that Lucifer was full of two things. What were these two things? ____________________

______________________________________________

4. Write out Ezekiel 28:15 in full: ______________

______________________________________________

______________________________________________

______________________________________________

5. What was found in Lucifer? ________________

______________________________________________

______________________________________________

6. How do we know Satan actually fell from heaven?

______________________________________________

______________________________________________

7. Who did he take with him when he fell? (Jude 6)

______________________________________________

8. Lucifer declared that he was going to do five things in Isaiah 14:13, 14. List all five things: __________

______________________________________________

______________________________________________

9. What satanic name and title do we find in Matthew 12:24? ______________________________

10. List four names for the enemy found in Revelation 12:9: ______________________________

______________________________________________

11. Who was the first sinner? ________________

12. Write out 1 John 3:8 in full: ______________

______________________________________________

______________________________________________

______________________________________________

______________________________________________

13. If you answered "Eve" to #11, does the above Scripture change your view? Why/Why not? ________

______________________________________________

14. Give four different names for demons found in the passages indicated:

1 Timothy 4:1 ______________________________

Mark 1:27 ________________________________

Luke 7:21 ________________________________

Lev. 20:6 ________________________________

15. What is awaiting these demons? (Jude 6) ______

________________________________________

16. Name two types of hindrances demons can cause (Matt. 12:22, 23): ______________________________

________________________________________

17. Read *and study* Matt. 8:28-34.

18. Write out Eph. 6:12 IN YOUR OWN WORDS:

________________________________________

________________________________________

________________________________________

19. Explain what this verse says to you: __________

________________________________________

________________________________________

________________________________________

20. Provide two Scripture references regarding demonic possession: ______________________________

________________________________________

21. Has Satan ever returned to heaven? (Job 1:6)

________________________________________

22. When asked where he had been, Satan answered, "From going to and fro in the earth, and from walking up and down in it." Job __ :___

23. Write out James 4:7 in full: ______________

________________________________________

________________________________________

________________________________________

________________________________________

24. Do you resist the devil? __________________

25. List three effective ways to resist the devil:

________________________________________

________________________________________

________________________________________

26. Read *and study* 2 Cor. 11:14.

27. Is there any way to defeat the devil? ________

________________________________________

28. Write a 200-250 word essay on Deut. 18:10-12 (Use separate page.)

29. The Bible describes several instances of Jesus casting out demons. Provide three examples of this:

________________________________________

________________________________________

________________________________________

30. The devil is stronger than any human being:

True or False

31. Write out 1 John 4:4 in full:______________

________________________________________

________________________________________

________________________________________

________________________________________

32. Where does a person get the strength to defeat Satan? (Phil. 4:13)________________________

________________________________________

33. Read *and study* Eph. 6:12.

34. Write out Luke 10:19 in full: ____________

________________________________________

________________________________________

________________________________________

35. Write out 1 John 5:18 IN YOUR OWN WORDS:

______________________________

______________________________

______________________________

______________________________

36. What is the name given to Satan in the following Scriptures?

Numbers 22:22______________________

Isaiah 14:12 ______________________

Matthew 4:3 ______________________

John 8:44 ______________________

Matthew 13:39 ______________________

2 Corinthians 6:15 ______________________

37. Can a person defeat Satan by knowing God's Word? Why/Why not?______________________

______________________________

______________________________

______________________________

38. "Beloved believe not every spirit but try the spirits whether they are from God." 1 ______ ___ :_____

39. Write out Isaiah 8:19 in full: ___________

______________________________

______________________________

______________________________

______________________________

40. In Daniel 10:13 we read about a demon which attempted to hinder Daniel's messenger from the Lord. In the spaces below provide:

a) The name of the demon and b) Number of days he was able to withstand God's angel.

a)______________________________

b)______________________________

41. Who tempted Jesus in the wilderness? (Matthew 4:1) ______________________________

42. Read Isaiah 8:19.

43. Does Isaiah 8:19 mean that it is acceptable or unacceptable to seek after familiar spirits? __________

______________________________

44. What is the message of Matthew 12:44, 45? ___

______________________________

______________________________

______________________________

45. Write out 1 Peter 5:8, 9 in full: ____________

______________________________

______________________________

______________________________

______________________________

______________________________

46. What is the message of 2 Corinthians 11:14?

______________________________

______________________________

______________________________

47. "Lord, even the devils are subject unto us through thy name." Luke ____ : _____

48. Read *and study* 2 Timothy 4:18. This is a very special promise. Be sure to claim it often.

49. In Mark 5:8, who said, "Come out of the man, thou unclean spirit?" ____________________

50. Write out Colossians 1:13 IN YOUR OWN WORDS. ______________________________

______________________________

______________________________

# APPENDIX F

# RESOURCES

Jack Roper, RN
C.A.R.I.S.
P.O. Box 1659
Milwaukee, WI 53201
(414) 771-7379

Personal Freedom Outreach
P.O. Box 26062
St. Louis, MO 63136
(314) 388-2648

Pat Pulling
B.A.D.D. (Bothered About
Dungeons & Dragons
P.O. Box 5513
Richmond, VA 23220
(804) 264-0403

Tipper Gore
Parents' Music Resource Center
1500 Arlington Blvd.
Arlington, VA 22209
(703) 527-9466

David C. DiCanio
American Christian Youth
P.O. Box 317
Collingswood, NJ 08108
(609) 665-3595

Carol Giambalvo
FOCUS
2567 Columbus Ave.
Oceanside, NY 11572

Cult Awareness Network
P.O. Box 608370
Chicago, IL 60626
(312) 267-7777

# Notes

## Chapter One

1. Jerry Johnston, *The Edge of Evil* (Dallas, TX: Word Publishing, 1989), 33.

## Chapter Two

1. Johanna Michaelsen, *Like Lambs to the Slaughter* (Eugene, OR: Harvest House Publishers, 1989), 241.
2. Kevin Marron, *Witches, Pagans, & Magic in the New Age* (Toronto: Seal Books, 1989), 253.

## Chapter Three

1. Larry Kahaner, *Cults That Kill* (New York: Warner Books, 1988), 183-185.
2. Ibid., 189.
3. Ibid., 6-7.
4. Johnston, *Edge of Evil*, 13.
5. Ibid.
6. Ibid., 2.
7. Ibid.
8. Ibid.
9. Ibid., 8.
10. Ibid.
11. Ibid., 62.
12. Ibid., 65.
13. Ibid., 66.
14. Kevin Marron, *Witches, Pagans, & Magic in the New Age* (Toronto: Seal Books, 1989), 193.
15. Ibid., 199.
16. Ibid., 200.
17. "Drugs, Satanic Movie, Murder," *Christian World Report.* Vol. 1, No. 1 (Sept 89): 11.

## Chapter Five

1. George Jonas, "A Cop's View of Kids," *Toronto Sun* (30 July 1990): 12.
2. Jerry Johnston, *The Edge of Evil* (Dallas, TX: Word Publishing, 1989), 124.

3. Ibid., 21.
4. James Wallace, "Satanic Junk 'A Threat to Kids,'" *Toronto Sun* (6 April 1990): 39.
5. Eric Barger, *From Rock to Rock* (Lafayette, LA: Huntington House Publishers, 1990), 179.
6. Duane Empey & Ted Schwarz, *Satanism* (Grand Rapids: Zondervan Books, 1988), 202.
7. Barger, *Rock to Rock*, 179-180.
8. Johnston, *Edge of Evil*, 19-20.

**Chapter Six**

1. From a personal letter to the author dated August 1990.
2. Duane Empey & Ted Schwarz, *Satanism* (Grand Rapids: Zondervan Books, 1988), 63-64.
3. Ibid., 196.
4. Jerry Johnston, *The Edge of Evil* (Dallas, TX: Word Publishing, 1989), 63.
5. Kevin Marron, *Witches, Pagans & Magic in the New Age* (Toronto: Seal Books, 1989), 10.
6. Patti LaLonde, "Satanism: A National Peril," *Christian World Report*, Vol 1, No. 1 (Feb. '89): 13-14.
7. Johnston, *Edge of Evil*, 163.
8. Marron, *Witches, Pagans & Magic*, 10.
9. Ibid., 115-116.
10. From a personal letter to the author dated August 1990.
11. Johanna Michaelsen, *Like Lambs to the Slaughter* (Eugene, OR: Harvest House Publishers, 1989), 193.
12. From a personal letter to the author from Jim Hardy dated 24 July 1990.
13. From a personal letter to the author dated August 1990.

**Chapter Seven**

1. Johanna Michaelsen, *Like Lambs to the Slaughter* (Eugene, OR: Harvest House Publishers, 1989), 263.
2. Copyright 1982 Last Days Ministries Box 40, Lindale, TX 75771-0040. All rights reserved. This article was reprinted from the *Last Days Magazine*. If you would like additional copies of it in tract form, please write to last Days Ministries at the above address and ask for LD #37. If you would like a sample of the *Last Days Magazine*, send your request to the same address.

## Chapter Eight

1. Dan and Steve Peters, *Why Knock Rock?* (Minneapolis: Bethany House Publishers, 1984), 91.
2. Nelson Price, *New Age, the Occult, and Lion Country* (Old Tappan, NJ: Power Books, 1989), 90.
3. Eric Barger, *From Rock to Rock* (Lafayette, LA: Huntington House Publishers, 1990), viii.
4. Ibid., 3-4.
5. Ibid., 45.
6. Ibid., 31.
7. Ibid.
8. Ibid., 101.
9. Peters, *Why Knock Rock*?, 94.
10. Ibid.
11. Barger, *Rock to Rock*, 130.
12. Ibid., 128.
13. Arthur Lyons, *Satan Wants You* (New York: Mysterious Press, 1988), 4.
14. Neil Perry, "Death Metal—Evil under the Sun," *Select* (March 1991):44.
15. Ibid., 42.
16. Steven Blush, "Grindcore," *Spin* (June 1991): 36.
17. Ryan Murphy, "Warning Labels Send Records up the Charts," *Cincinnatti Enquirer* (6 September 1989).
18. Richard H.P. Sia, "Zappa Performs Solo Before Legislators to Urge Defeat of Obscene-Music Bill." *The Baltimore Sun* (19 March 1986).
19. Bill Holland, "Md. Senate Holds Hearing on Porno Bill," *Billboard Magazine*. (29 March 1986).
20. Barger, *Rock to Rock*, 175.

## Chapter Nine

1. Pat Pulling, *The Devil's Web* (Lafayette, LA: Huntington House Publishers, 1989), 80.
2. Philip Bonewitz, *Authentic Thaumaturgy: A Professional Occultist on Improving the Realism of Magic Systems in Fantasy Stimulation Games* (Berkeley, CA: Chaosium, Inc., 1980).
3. From the rule book for the game Arduin Grimoire, Vol. 1:60
4. Advanced Dungeons & Dragons Player's Handbook, 31.
5. Advanced Dungeons & Dragons Master's Guide, 15.

6. Advanced Dungeons & Dragons Handbook, 33.
7. Pat Pulling, *The Devil's Web*, (Lafayette, LA: Huntington House Publishers, 1989), 100-101.

**Chapter Ten**

1. Eric Barger, *From Rock to Rock* (Lafayette, LA: Huntington House Publishers, 1990), 30.

# *confessions of a*
# *TEENAGE SATANIST*

"I stared into the flickering black candle that sat in the midst of the skull and black-handled knives on my home made altar to Satan. Reciting the incantation, I tried to ignore my nagging thoughts. *I was still young—just a teenager. How had I come to the place where I felt like I was sliding headfirst into hell?"*

**Charles Evans best-selling tract, *Confessions of a Teenage Satanist*, recounts his youthful involvement with Satanism.**

". . . during . . . boring Sunday church services I wondered, 'Is this all there is to knowing God?' . . . I soon rebelled against church and simply stopped going. . . ."

**Discover a message that compels teenagers from all over North America to write to the author pleading for help in getting out of their dead-end involvement with Satanism.**

"I wondered if [the] 'god' of the rock bands was what I had been searching for! . . . Soon I had a personal library on the black arts and a huge 'circle of salt' on the basement floor at home. . . . I wore an upside-down cross outside my black T-shirt, which proudly proclaimed, 'Satan lives!' . . . Instead of finding the pathway to God, I was sliding headfirst into the depths of hell."

**Pass along the truth about Satanism exposed in this tract and help some teenager find the Way to escape this miserable lifestyle.**

". . . helplessly trapped . . . I poured out my heart to God. . . . [He] freed me from Satan and changed my life forever . . . if He can save a teenage devil worshipper like me, He can save you too."

*For more information about the American Tract Society or to order copies of this or other tracts, write to the following: American Tract Society • Box 462008 • Garland, TX 75046 • USA*

# More Good Books From Huntington House Publishers

***Blessings of Liberty: Restoring the City on the Hill***
by Charles Heath

The author believes that Liberalism is destroying our nation. If we continue to do nothing, says Heath, the traditional family values that we cherish and the kind of government envisioned by our founding fathers will cease to exist. Heath presents a coherent case for limited government, decentralized and self-governing communities, and a return to traditional values. Conservatism, he asserts, has its premise in Genesis; it is the only viable philosophy capable of addressing and solving today's problems.

**ISBN 1-56384-005-7 $8.95 Trade paper**
**ISBN 1-56384-007-3 $16.95 Hardcover**

***En Route to Global Occupation*** by Gary Kah

High ranking government liaison Gary Kah warns that national sovereignty will soon be a thing of the past. Political forces around the world are now cooperating in unprecedented fashion to achieve their goal of uniting the people of this planet under a New World Order. The author demonstrates, displaying reproductions of the original documents calling for and implementing the plans for a world constitution and government, that there is an ominous cooperation between the globalists, who are promoting the one world government, and the burgeoning New Age groups in America, who are promoting a new religion. Kah was dismissed from his position after being warned by a top level government agency to "Keep Quiet" about the globalists' activities; he continues to lecture and expose their plans.

**ISBN 1-56384-005-7 $8.95 Trade paper**
**ISBN 1-56384-007-3 $16.95 Hardcover**

***Cover of Darkness (A Novel)*** by J. Carroll

Jack's time is running out. The network's top investigative reporter has been given the most bizarre and difficult assignment of his life. The powers behind the conspiracy (occult and demonic forces) are finally exposed by Jack. Now comes the real challenge—convincing others. Matching wits with supernatural forces, Jack faces the most hideous conspiracy the world has ever known.

**ISBN 0-910311-31-5 $7.95**

***The Image of the Ages*** by David Webber

Are the secular humanists' plans for a New World Order about to be realized? How will the establishment of this order affect you and your family? David Webber, author of *The Image of the Ages*, explains how modern technology, artificial intelligence, and other scientific advances will be used in the near future to manipulate and control the masses.

**ISBN 0-910311-38-2 $7.95**

***Psychic Phenomena Unveiled: Confessions of a New Age Warlock*** by John Anderson

He walked on hot coals and stopped his heart. As one of Los Angeles' most recognized psychics, John Anderson was on top of the world. His ability to perform psychic phenomena converted the most stubborn unbeliever into a true believer in occult power. But John Anderson sensed his involvement in the occult was destroying him. This book was written to expose the trickery behind the New Age magic and address man's attraction to the occult.

**ISBN 0-910311-49-8 $8.95**

***Who Will Rule the Future?*** by Paul McGuire

Film producer-turned-author, Paul McGuire, says: "There are powerful political and spiritual forces that are attempting to usher in a New Age theocracy, promote a New World Order, and control our nation." Is the Christian community ignoring its responsibility to oppose these forces? Christians have retreated from society and abdicated their responsibility. In the next few years, we will pay a heavy price for our neglect. This book calls Christians to move powerfully into our society and confront the direction of our culture before it's too late!

**ISBN 0-910311-94-3 $8.95**

***Crystalline Connection (A Novel)***
by Bob Maddux & Mary Carpenter Reid

Enter the enchanting World of Ebbern, a planet in many ways like our own. In the *Crystalline Connection* our hero, Bracken, returns to his homeland after ten years of wandering. Once there he becomes involved in a monumental struggle gallantly confronting the dark forces of evil. This futuristic fantasy is fraught with intrigue, adventure, romance and much more. The *Crystalline Connection* artfully discloses the devastating consequences of involvement in the New Age movement while using the medium of fiction.

**ISBN 0-910311-71-4 $8.95**

***"Soft Porn" Plays Hardball*** by Dr. Judith A. Reisman

With amazing clarity, the author demonstrates that pornography imposes on society a view of women and children that encourages violence and sexual abuse. As crimes against women and children increase to alarming proportions, it's of paramount importance that we recognize the cause of this violence. Pornography should be held accountable for the havoc it has wreaked in our homes and our country.

**ISBN 0-910311-65-X $8.95 Trade paper**
**ISBN 0-910311-92-7 $16.95 Hardcover**

***Kinsey, Sex and Fraud: The Indoctrination of a People***
by Dr. Judith A. Reisman and Edward Eichel

*Kinsey, Sex and Fraud* describes the research of Alfred Kinsey which shaped Western society's beliefs and understanding of the nature of human sexuality. His unchallenged conclusions are taught at every level of education and quoted in textbooks as undisputed truth.

The authors clearly demonstrate that Kinsey's research involved illegal experimentations on several hundred children. The survey was carried out on a non-representative group of Americans, including disproportionately large numbers of sex offenders, prostitutes, prison inmates and exhibitionists.

**ISBN 0-910311-20-X $19.95 Hardcover**

***Seduction of the Innocent Revisited***
by John Fulce

You honestly can't judge a book by its cover—especially a comic book! Comic books of yesteryear bring to mind cute cartoon characters, super-heroes battling the forces of evil or a sleuth tracking down the bad guy clue-by-clue. But that was a long, long time ago.

Today's comic books aren't innocent at all! Author John Fulce asserts that "super-heroes" are constantly found in the nude engaging in promiscuity, and satanic symbols are abundant throughout the pages. Fulce says most parents aren't aware of the contents of today's comic books. Comic books are *not* as innocent as they used to be.

**ISBN 0-910311-66-8 $8.95**

***Dinosaurs and the Bible*** by David W. Unfred

Every reader, young and old, will be fascinated by this ever-mysterious topic—exactly what happened to the dinosaurs? Author David Unfred draws a very descriptive picture of the history and fate of the dinosaurs, using the Bible as a reference guide.

In this educational and informative book, Unfred answers such questions as: Did dinosaurs really exist? Does the Bible mention dinosaurs? What happened to dinosaurs, or are there some still living awaiting discovery? Unfred uses the Bible to help unlock the ancient mysteries of the lumbering creatures, and teaches how those mysteries can educate us about God the Creator and our God of Love.

**ISBN 0-910311-70-6 $12.95 Hardcover**

***God's Rebels*** by Henry Lee Curry III

From his unique perspective Dr. Henry Lee Curry III offers a fascinating look at the lives of some of our greatest Southern religious leaders during the Civil War. The rampant Evangelical Christianity prominent at the outbreak of the Civil War, asserts Dr. Curry, is directly traceable to the 2nd Great Awakening of the early 1800s. The evangelical tradition, with its emphasis on strict morality, individual salvation, and emotional worship, had influenced most of Southern Protestantism by this time. Southerners unquestionably believed the voice of the ministers to be the "voice of God"; consequently, the church became one of the most powerful forces influencing Confederate life. Inclined toward a Calvinistic emphasis on predestination, the South was confident that God would sustain its way of life.

**ISBN: 0-910311-67-6 $12.95 Trade paper**
**ISBN: 0-910311-68-4 $21.95 Hardcover**

***Inside the New Age Nightmare*** by Randall Baer

Now, for the first time, one of the most powerful and influential leaders of the New Age movement has come out to expose the deceptions of the organization he once led. New Age magazines and articles have for many years hailed Randall Baer as their most "radically original" and "advanced" thinker... "light years ahead of others" says leading New Age magazine *East-West Journal*. His bestselling books on quartz crystals, self-transformation, and planetary ascension have won worldwide acclaim and been extolled by New Agers from all walks of life.

Hear, from a New Age insider, the secret plans they have spawned to take over our public, private, and political institutions. Turned from darkness to light, Randall Baer reveals the methods of the New Age movement as no one else can. Find out what you can do to stop the New Age movement from destroying our way of life.

**ISBN 0-910311-58-7 $8.95**

***From Rock to Rock*** by Eric Barger

Over three years in the making, the pages of this book represent thousands of hours of detailed research as well as over twenty-six years of personal experience and study.The author presents a detailed exposé on many current rock entertainers, rock concerts, videos, lyrics and occult symbols used within the industry. He also presents a rating system of over fifteen hundred past and present rock groups and artists.

**ISBN 0-910311-61-7 $8.95**

***The Deadly Deception: Freemasonry Exposed By One of Its Top Leaders*** by Tom McKenney

Presents a frank look at Freemasonry and its origin. Learn of the "secrets" and "deceptions" that are practiced daily around the world. Find out why Masonry teaches that it is the true religion, that all other religions are but corrupted and perverted forms of Masonry.

**ISBN 0-910311-54-4 $7.95**

***Lord! Why Is My Child a Rebel?*** by Jacob Aranza

This book offers an analysis of the root causes of teenage rebellion and offers practical solutions for disoriented parents. Aranza focuses on the turbulent teenage years, and how to survive those years—both you and the child! Must reading for parents—especially for those with strong-willed children. This book will help you avoid the traps in which many parents are caught and put you on the road to recovery with your teenager.

**ISBN 0-910311-62-5 $6.95**

***New World Order: The Ancient Plan of Secret Societies*** by William Still

Secret societies such as Freemasons have been active since before the advent of Christ, yet most of us don't realize what they are or the impact they've had on many historical events. Author William Still brings into focus the actual manipulative work of the societies, and the "Great Plan" they follow, much to the surprise of many of those who are blindly led into the organization. Their ultimate goal is simple: world dictatorship and unification of all mankind into a world confederation.

It is a struggle between two foes—the forces of religion versus the forces of anti-religion. Still asserts that although the final battle is near-at-hand, the average person has the power to thwart the efforts of secret societies. Startling and daring, this is the first successful attempt by an author to unveil the designs of secret societies from the beginning, up to the present and into the future. The author attempts to educate the community on how to recognize the signals and how to take the necessary steps to impede their progress.

**ISBN 0-910311-64-1 $8.95**

***Hidden Dangers of the Rainbow*** by Constance Cumbey

The first book to uncover and expose the New Age movement, this national #1 bestseller paved the way for all other books on the subject became a giant in its category. This book provides a vivid exposé of the New Age movement, which the author contends is dedicated to wiping out Christianity and establishing a one world order. This movement, a vast network of occult and pagan organizations, meets the test of prophecy concerning the Antichrist.

**ISBN 0-910311-03-X $8.95**

***To Grow By Storybook Readers*** by Janet Friend

Today the quality of education is a major concern; consequently, more and more parents have turned to home schooling to teach their children how to read. The *To Grow By Storybook Readers* by Janet Friend can greatly enhance your home schooling reading program. The set of readers consists of 18 storybook readers plus 2 activity books. The *To Grow By Storybook Readers* has been designed to be used in conjunction with Marie LeDoux's PLAY 'N TALK phonics program but will work well with other orderly phonics programs.

These are the first phonics readers that subtly but positively instill scriptural and moral values. They're a joy to use because no prior instructional experience is necessary. The *To Grow By Storybook Readers* allows parents and children to work together learning each sound. Your child progresses through the readers and learns to appreciate his own ability to understand and think logically about word and sentence construction, thereby raising his self-esteem and confidence.

**ISBN 0-910311-69-2 $44.95 per set**

***Personalities in Power: The Making of Great Leaders***
by Florence Littauer

You'll laugh and cry as Florence Littauer shares with you heart-warming accounts of the personal lives of some of our greatest leaders. Learn of their triumphs and tragedies, and become aware of the different personality patterns that exist and how our leaders have been influenced by them. Discover your own strengths and weaknesses by completing the

Personality Chart included in this book. *Personalities in Power* lets you understand yourself and others and helps you live up to your full potential.
**ISBN 0-910311-56-0 $8.95**

***The Last Days Collection*** by Last Days Ministries

Heart-stirring, faith-challenging messages from Keith Green, David Wilkerson, Melody Green, Leonard Ravenhill, Winkie Pratney, Charles Finney and William Booth are designed to awaken complacent Christians to action.

**ISBN 0-961-30020-5 $8.95**

***The Lucifer Connection*** by Joseph Carr

Shirley MacLaine and other celebrities are persuading millions that the New Age movement can fill the spiritual emptiness in their lonely lives. Joseph Carr explains why the New Age movement is the most significant and potentially destructive challenge to the church today. But is it new? How should Christians protect themselves and their children from this insidious threat? This book is a prophetic, information-packed examination by one of the most informed authors in America.

**ISBN 0-910311-42-0 $7.95**

***Exposing the AIDS Scandal: What You Don't Know Can Kill You*** by Dr. Paul Cameron

Where do you turn when those who control the flow of information in this country withhold the truth? Why is the national media hiding facts from the public? Can AIDS be spread in ways we're not being told? Finally a book that gives you a total account of the AIDS epidemic, and what steps can be taken to protect yourself. What you don't know can kill you!

**ISBN 0-910311-52-8 $7.95**

***America Betrayed*** by Marlin Maddoux

This hard-hitting book exposes the forces in our country which seek to destroy the family, the schools and our values. This book details exactly how the news media manipulates your mind. Marlin Maddoux is the host of the popular, national radio talk show "Point of View."

**ISBN 0-910311-18-8 $6.95**

***Devil Take the Youngest*** by Winkie Pratney

A history of Satan's hatred of innocence and his historical treachery against the young. Pratney begins his journey in ancient Babylon and continues through to modern-day America where infants are murdered daily and children are increasingly victimized through pornography, prostitution and humanism.

**ISBN 0-910311-29-3 $8.95**